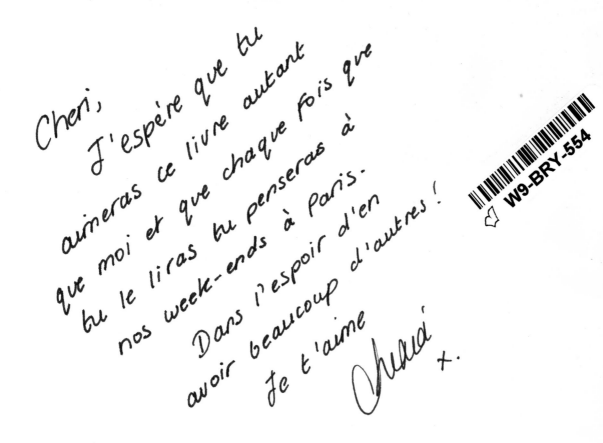

Cheri,

J'espère que tu aimeras ce livre autant que moi et que chaque fois que tu le liras tu penseras à nos week-ends à Paris.

Dans l'espoir d'en avoir beaucoup d'autres !

Je t'aime

x.

THE PARIS CAFÉ COOKBOOK

Rendezvous and

Recipes from

50 Best Cafés

THE Paris Café COOKBOOK

Daniel Young

Photography by Sophie Elmosnino
Illustrations by Camille Joste

William Morrow and Company, Inc. New York

For Mitch Brower and David Brower

Library of Congress Cataloging-in-Publication Data
Young, Daniel.
The Paris café cookbook / Daniel Young; photography
by Sophie Elmosnino; illustrations by Camille Joste.
p.   cm.
Includes index.
ISBN 0-688-15330-5
1. Cookery, French.   2. Restaurants—France—
Paris—Guidebooks.   I. Title.
TX719.Y68   1998
641.5944—dc21   98-2840
                                                                                        CIP

Printed in the United States of America

First Edition

3   4   5   6   7   8   9   10

BOOK DESIGN BY RICHARD ORIOLO

www.williammorrow.com

ACKNOWLEDGMENTS

The rendezvous, reveries, and recipes revealed in this book owe their cinematic character and epicurean allure to the many extraordinary personalities I had the pleasure of meeting, or merely observing, on both sides of the café *comptoir*. But this and every other café romantic should first thank the crews working behind and amid the action for making everything possible. I am especially indebted to the *garçons, serveuses,* cooks, chefs, and keepers of the fifty featured cafés for first treating me no worse—and certainly no better—than any other habitué, itself a great honor, and later for being so cooperative and candid once they discovered what I was up to.

I feel most fortunate to have worked with photographer Sophie Elmosnino and illustrator Camille Joste, two perceptive *parisiennes* who met me at dozens of cafés, humored my more foolish whims, and greatly enhanced my vision for a very personal and nuanced compilation of café moods and foods. I am also grateful to Anne Trager for testing and clarifying many of the chefs' recipes as well as enduring my panic attacks and to my good pals Tamara Holt, Teresa Thompson, JoAnn Makovitzky, Marco Moreira, and Daniel Orr for their cooking assistance and suggestions.

Heartfelt thanks to David Brower and Agnès Lozet, whose generosity, conviviality, and laughter awaited me in Paris as steadfastly as the Eiffel Tower. They were the first links in a long chain of momentous introductions, extending from the garrulous bistro connoisseur Patrick Pougeux, whose ardent thirsts turned the most routine rendezvous into grand occasions, to Alain Weill, the gourmet dandy who, through his unrelenting criticism, encouraged me to take a stand, however unfashionable or unreasonable it might be, and defend it.

Mercis to David Downie and Alison Harris, for their invaluable friendship, advice, and thoughtfulness as well as their great wit and *bon gout;* to my cousin Philomène Grandin, for acting as my accomplice on numerous Parisian eating adventures; and to Christel Lozet, for her confidence in this project and her classy, charming company. I also profited enormously from the companionship and insights of Gérard-Georges Lemaire, Luc Bertin, Chantal Pougeux, Juliette Joste, Maguy Tordjman, Veronique Naël, Pasquale Noizet, Brigitte Barnaud, Chloé Dubois-Violette, Pierre Bercut, Héléne Bontemps, Mary Hyman, Philip Hyman, Antoine Jaubert, Jean-Pierre Lyonnet, François Blanc, Virginie Collot, Guiseppe Bovo, Marie Naël, Philippe Loiseaux, André Blanc, Bernard Lheritier, and Louisa Cheref.

In New York I had the unwavering support of my parents, who must know they are never far from my heart; my friends Mitch Brower, Mark Giles, Arthur Schwartz, Monica Forrestall, Alan Cohen, Steven Forbis, Leslie Laurence, Anne de Ravel, Jeff Weinstein, Mary Barone, Richard Schreiber, June Rogoznica, Julia Martin, Leonard Lopate, Diana Biederman, and Nina Blaine; my cousin Marilyn Goodman; and my *Daily News* editors Larry Hackett, Rosemary Black, and Jane Freiman. I also enjoyed the backing of my brothers, Bill and Roy; my sisters-in-law, Laurie and Sharon; and my nieces, Elizabeth, Molly, Hava, and Shoshana.

My deepest appreciation to my agent and staunch advocate Alice Martell, whose great smarts, style, toughness, and humor are awfully nice to have in your corner. I am also proud of my association with the cookbook pros at William Morrow and, in particular, my shrewd and purposeful editor Justin Schwartz. I am thankful too for Ann Cahn's sensitive eye in guiding this project from manuscript to bound book; for Richard Oriolo's resourceful layout; for Karen Lumley's beautiful production work; and for the help of Cara Anselmo and Christy Stabin in getting through the day-to-day dilemmas.

Finally, a warm embrace to everyone I met in Paris who heard my overture, *"venez prendre le café avec moi,"* "come have a coffee with me," and said, "O.K."

CONTENTS

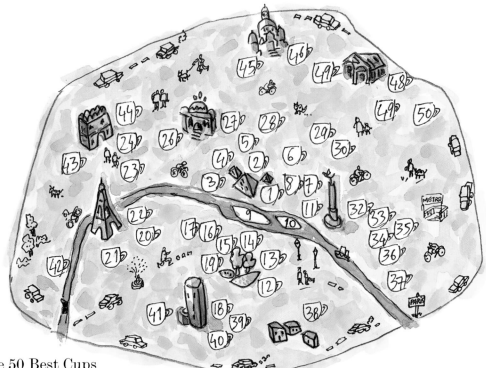

The 50 Best Cups in Paris

First Arrondissement

1. Aux Tonneaux des Halles: 28, rue Montorgueil
2. Le Café Marly: 93, rue de Rivoli
3. Café Véry: Jardin des Tuileries
4. Bar de l'Entracte: 47, rue de Montpensier

Second Arrondissement

5. Le Vaudeville: 29, rue Vivienne

Third Arrondissement

6. Web Bar: 32, rue de Picardie

Fourth Arrondissement

7. Dame Tartine: 2, rue Brisemiche
8. Café Beaubourg: 100, rue St-Martin
9. Brasserie des Deux Palais: 3, boulevard du Palais
10. Brasserie de l'Île St-Louis: 55, quai de Bourbon
11. Ma Bourgogne: 19, place des Vosges

Fifth Arrondissement

12. Les Fontaines: 9, rue Soufflot
13. Brasserie Balzar: 49, rue des Écoles

Sixth Arrondissement

14. Bouillon Racine: 3, rue Racine
15. Brasserie Lipp: 151, boulevard St-Germain
16. Aux Deux Magots: 170, boulevard St-Germain

17. Café de Flore: 172, boulevard St-Germain
18. Le Sélect: 99, boulevard Montparnasse
19. Brasserie Lutétia: 23, rue de Sèvres

Seventh Arrondissement

20. Café Rako: 34, rue St-Dominique
21. Café du Marché: 38, rue Cler
22. La Poule au Pot: 121, rue de l'Université

Eighth Arrondissement

23. Café Blanc: 40, rue François-1er
24. Fouquet's: 99, avenue des Champs-Élysées
25. Chez Léon: 5, rue de l'Isly

Ninth Arrondissement

26. Café de la Paix: 12, boulevard des Capucines
27. Au Général La Fayette: 52, rue La Fayette

Tenth Arrondissement

28. Le Petit Château-d'Eau: 34, rue Château d'Eau

Eleventh Arrondissement

29. Café Cannibale: 93, rue Jean-Pierre-Timbaud
30. Café Charbon: 109, rue Oberkampf
31. Clown Bar: 114, rue Amelot
32. Café de l'Industrie: 16, rue St-Sabin
33. Pause Café: 41, rue de Charonne
34. Le Bistrot du Peintre: 116, avenue Ledru-Rollin
35. Aux Petits Joueurs: 8, rue de la Main-d'Or

Twelfth Arrondissement

36. L'Ébauchoir: 43–45, rue de Cîteaux
37. Le Viaduc Café: 43, avenue Daumesnil

Thirteenth Arrondissement

38. Chez Gladines: 30, rue des Cinq-Diamants

Fourteenth Arrondissement

39. La Coupole: 102, boulevard Montparnasse
40. Café de la Place: 23, rue d'Odessa

Fifteenth Arrondissement

41. Au Roi du Café: 59, rue Lecourbe

Sixteenth Arrondissement

42. Zébra Square: 3, place Clément-Ader
43. Brasserie Stella: 133, avenue Victor-Hugo

Seventeenth Arrondissement

44. Pétrissans: 30 bis, avenue Niel

Eighteenth Arrondissement

45. Le Sancerre: 35, rue des Abbesses
46. L'Été en Pente Douce: 23, rue Muller

Nineteenth Arrondissement

47. Le Rendez-vous des Quais: 10, quai de la Seine
48. Café de la Musique: 221, avenue Jean-Jaurès

Twentieth Arrondissement

49. Zéphyr: 1, rue du Jourdain
50. Flèche d'Or Café: 102 bis, rue de Bagnolet

INTRODUCTION

I maintain that it is essential to have a regular café," wrote Robert Doisneau, photographer laureate of the Parisian bistro. "Two would even be better."

Possession of two cafés solves, among other situational dilemmas, the stalemate faced by estranged lovers willing to cede all shared resources save for a cherished bistro, traditionally the last refuge of the unattached, the unemployed, or the otherwise unappreciated. Who would dare sacrifice, at such times, the indulgent comforts of a caned or hardwood seat contoured expressly for the Parisian soul (if not derrière)?

Move that same chair outside the Paris periphery and it's nothing but old furniture. A foreigner longing for consolation and inspiration might purchase it at a premium from an antiques dealer, but he would still be missing all the things that make a café special. Chairs and tables do not transform scribblers and doodlers into poets and painters. But looks, words, thoughts, emo-

tions, warmth, wine, and good food sometimes do, especially when experienced and exchanged at one of the many coffee-brewing beacons in the City of Light.

These are the people-percolating properties I have tried to bring home through this collection of favorite café recipes and rendezvous. In the most richly rendered portrayals of Parisian café life you can practically taste the flavors of a favorite hangout. My raison d'être as a vagabond searching for fifty cafés you might, when in Paris, want to call home has been to trim off the "practically," to capture the character *and* taste, down to the last ingredient, of these adored haunts. Rather than create a still portrait of Paris as a museum, the aim has been to piece together a richly flavored collage of a historically vibrant city in constant motion. Its dateline is the Paris living in this fin-de-siècle and not in the storied one a century ago.

The French term *café*, in the larger sense,

can be applied to any establishment where you can stop in for nothing more than a beverage and stay for as long as you like. That all-important distinction explains why all bistros are not cafés, though the two designations are often used interchangeably. To be considered a café, a bistro must welcome, at least during specified hours, those who want only a glass of wine or a cup of coffee. Bistros that open their doors exclusively for lunches and dinners can take after restaurants more than they do cafés. Indeed, the confusion, when it arises, usually comes from fashionable restaurants that call themselves bistros, since the stylish designation makes them sound both cozy and sophisticated, though they lack the humble, homey, and hospitable virtues of the bistro soul.

Brasseries, too, qualify as cafés, no matter their elegance, if some of their tables can be occupied solely for the consumption of beverages. The famous brasserie La Coupole is therefore a café; Boffinger is not. The term *brasserie*, from the word *brasseur* (brewer), originally indicated establishments that served beer. But now it specifies grand café-restaurants offering continuous service and, as a result, rough-and-ready food. Brasseries specialize in dishes that can be cooked quickly (*sole meunière*, steaks), in advance (*gigot d'agneau rôti*—roast leg of lamb, *choucroute garnie*—sauerkraut with meats), or not at all (steak tartare, raw oysters) and don't need to be constantly fussed over by a highly skilled chef. These are the same attributes that make café cooking so practical and doable for the home cook.

Among the other French words used to indicate a café are *bougnat* (coal merchant), *troquet* (keeper of a café), *estaminet* (small café), *buvette* (refreshment bar), *tabac* or *café-tabac* (tobacconist), and *zinc* (for the tin-plated counters wrongly believed to be made of zinc). A possessive habitué may instead call a favorite rendezvous *"mon annexe"* (my annex), *"mon deuxième chez moi"* (my second home), *"mon Q.G."* (my *quartier général*, or headquarters), at least until the bill collectors arrive. Often he recalls only the street of a place he's frequented hundreds of times. "Meet me," he'll alert your answering machine, "at my Q.G. on the rue Daguerre," oblivious to the half dozen other cafés on that same street.

In the hometown of the Louvre, the Eiffel Tower, Notre-Dame, and their gastronomic counterparts, there is no institution so monumental to its cultural identity, both real and imagined, as the local café. Among enclosed spaces, it animates a greater range of rhythms and moods than cinema, opera house, art museum, church, office, classroom, kitchen, even boudoir. To cross its threshold, itself one of an estimated 2,800 power outlets in a great municipal utility, is to be plugged in to the inner dialogue of the French capital. That entrance, routine as it is to natives, is instant access to a million story lines, maybe even that one-in-a-million romance. At a Right Bank café, I naively asked filmmaker Claude Chabrol, the founder of the French New Wave, if finding the love of your life in a café was a realistic hope or only a romanticized fiction. "In a café, anything is possible," he responded, "including that nothing will happen."

The café, I came to discover, is about possibilities revealed by way of contrasts. Resplendent in full color yet most provocative in black and white, it's an improvisational drama that sparkles of champagne one day and bicarbonate of soda the next. Through its doors pass young aristocrats and old radicals, curious locals and blasé foreigners, famous writers and obscure painters, sober comedians and frivolous accountants, serene teenagers and raucous widows, early-bird boozers and closing-time teetotalers, analytical waiters and philosophical proprietors.

The regulars come for solitude, relaxation, and a daydreamy seat at a quiet table in the *salle* (dining room) on Tuesday; then company, stimulation, and a standing squeeze at the "zinc" *comptoir* (counter/bar) on Thursday. Many rendezvous are planned; others occur by chance, unless you believe, as Left Bank romantics do, there is no such thing as chance. Such café encounters are, as the French say, *déjà écrit*—already written.

Outside, the café terrace is an emotional panorama of inspiration and confusion, celebration and consolation, romance and estrangement, division and reconciliation. It's always impossible to tell who has the best views. Is it the poseurs settled into caned chairs, their necks all craned toward the sun as if in a field of sunflowers, their eyes ostensibly poring over their *Le Mondes*, their Filofaxes, their companions? Or is it the passersby facing in, their heads expertly turned to give the café throng the look? Regardless, one without the other is Cleveland. Well, not quite.

Naturally, the best cafés must satisfy appetites, thirsts, and other daily desires that are felt, if not always spoken, in French. Inside cramped kitchens, the ranges, grills, deep-fryers, ovens, toasters, and, all too often, microwaves are in overdrive from the time of the first short coffee of the morning until the last long cocktail of the evening, warming croissants and *pains chocolats*, baking tourtes and fruit tarts, slow-cooking soups and stews, roasting chicken and lamb, sautéing fish and potatoes, pan-frying steaks and omelets, melting Gruyère over *croque monsieur* sandwiches and French onion soup, boiling eggs for the great bistro standard *oeufs mayonnaise* (hard-boiled eggs and mayo).

In a dark corner by the dessert table, a handyman nervously watches the last lonely wedge of perfectly caramelized *tarte Tatin* (upside-down apple pie), hoping that forlorn remainder will stick around and make its way to his table. When the waitress serves it to him, he beams. But when she puts out another pristine tart, he pouts. He prefers something newer, something fresher. Such is the character of the Parisian man, as the Parisian woman knows all too well.

Most of the affordable fare served at cafés could be described as French home cooking if as many as one in five French people still ate that way at home. But contemporary Parisians in particular lack the time, money, and energy for traditional, made-from-scratch meals. Sunday family meals are less often practiced than they are lamented during express lunches and frozen dinners. Meanwhile, the restaurant tabs at the city's gastronomic temples seem further beyond the reach of average folks than ever before.

These changes and their consequences have positioned the old-fashioned café, an endangered species disappearing in France at the rate of four hundred per year, for a comeback. Old bistros and brasseries and the new retro cafés inspired by them are all the rage in Paris. Their quick service and affordable prices appeal to budget-crunched Parisians. Their traditional, mom's-food-like *plats du jour*, vintage decor, and cozy seating arrangements satisfy widespread nostalgia for an easier time. "Zinc," which is to say tin, is once again proving to be the best conductor of human warmth. New or restored tin-plated bars are on back order at Ateliers Nectoux, one of two Parisian firms left in the trade.

In the past, cafés thrived in large part by giving Parisians, permanent or transient, what they couldn't get at home. During the boom years between 1860 and 1896, when the city's population nearly doubled from 1,280,000 to 2,500,000, that often meant offering a glass of wine, a hot meal, temporary shelter, and a sense of belonging to the new arrivals, many of them workingmen who'd left their wives and families behind in the provinces. (The literary cafés would soon do the same for expatriate artists.) Until World War II, they were the only places you could get a cold beverage. After the war and the advent of the household refrigerator, cafés endured as the sole outlets for espresso-style coffee. Now that espresso machines are everywhere, a growing number of cafés accustomed to serving only stale sandwiches, hot dogs, and tired-looking

charcuterie (much of the café fare could indeed be *dégueu*—short for *dégueulasse*, or disgusting) are recognizing that home cooking is something many Parisians no longer get at home.

Even affluent gourmands who can easily afford $100 lunches and $200 dinners are yearning for something homier. Much of 1990s haute cuisine has grown too calculated, too complicated, too impersonal. Like the worst of the serious modern architecture, it is fashioned to be admired first and used second. The decade's culinary masterpieces, though designed by individuals of singular talent, too often resemble the end product of an assembly line of cooks and high-tech machinery rather than the oeuvre of a human chef with moods, whims, and passions. What's served at the table is as much processed image as it is fresh food.

One positive response has been a push toward *cuisine du marché*—"market cuisine"—in which top-rated chefs shop for inspiration. Their latest dishes and menus are inspired by the freshest, highest-quality seasonal ingredients available at the Rungis wholesale market. This is nothing new within the bistro subculture, where one's ability to procure the best regional meats, cheeses, seafood, and produce is exalted over one's talent to prepare them. But it is astounding in this age of culinary celebrities to see multistarred chefs behaving as though the product, and not themselves, were king.

Which isn't to say their ingenuity is insignificant, nor that their influence is minimal. Several contemporary-minded café chefs are beneficiaries of trickle-down gastronomics. They adapt, simplify, and personalize trends in French culinary arts, fusing, for example, Asian spices (coriander, curry, ginger, cumin) or Arab staples (couscous, harissa, tahini) into their daily specials. Christophe Barnier of Café Cannibale takes the paper-thin pastry for Tunisian *bricks* and experiments with a wide variety of fillings, as world-famous chefs have done with filo as their format. Café de la Paix's Christian Le Squer, who cooked in the celebrated kitchens of Lucas Carton and Taillevent, instead uses *kadaifi,* a Middle Eastern dough, to give his *acras de morue* (salt cod croquettes) a crisp, shredded-wheat-like coating. Another Taillevent alumnus, Robert Petit, who also worked under such highly respected chefs as Bernard Fournier and Jacques Maximin, accents his sauces for $7.50 salmon dishes at Café Véry with the likes of coconut milk, mint, curry, and ginger. His former colleagues visit often and take mental notes.

Taken collectively, the recipes I have accumulated from fifty café chefs constitute a sidewalk-level introduction to—and review of—both classic and contemporary French cooking. With that objective always in mind, dishes were also chosen for their straightforward appeal and their accessibility to the American palate and shopper. Dishes that require ingredients not readily available in U.S. markets were eliminated from consideration when suitable substitutions could not be identified.

Although few of the recipes could be described as "low in fat," who's to say the café diet won't help Americans lose weight? Parisian men and women who follow a non-nonfat course still manage to maintain through their adult lives the waistlines and hip spans of fourteen-year-olds. While smoking habits, wine consumption, and congenital traits must also contribute to their bookmark-shaped bodies, I'm convinced that moderation and balance are the keys to their thinner ways. We diet-conscious Americans ban fats from our diet, ignoring how much flavor (and therefore pleasure) is absorbed and stored in a tablespoon of killer butter, a quarter cup of murderous cream, or a single lethal egg yolk, and how many more calories reside in a half-pound serving of healthy pasta. The trend in France is to savor several things in small quantities, to eat for flavor and balance rather than volume. Indeed, the French are masters of small indulgences (cognac, perfume, stolen kisses). They believe that if you eat something with pleasure, it will not harm you. When you force yourself to eat something, you risk being unhealthy. Nice philosophy, *non?*

The featured cafés were chosen for their food first and then for their owners, clientele, ambience, architecture, location, and history and how these all reflect the personality of the many small, independently minded communities within Paris. Several noteworthy cafés, including Café des Phares, La Palette, and a personal favorite, Café de la Mairie (at place St-Sulpice), were regrettably eliminated due to their limited menus. Among trendy hangouts—Café Cannibale, Café Charbon, Pause Café, the Louvre's Le Café Marly—I have tried my best to include only those with staying power, or, at the very least, those that deserve to stick around. The overall intention has been to cover as wide a description of café pleasures and styles as possible.

Nevertheless, the selection is very personal and could not have been assembled by a native of Paris inured to its charms and loyal to, at most, a handful of its haunts. Rather, the places were singled out by me, a spellbound New Yorker desperate to know which of his café infatuations had the stuff of true love. Not just for me, but also for persons whose backgrounds, temperaments, interests, preferences, and objectives are different from my own. *Chacun son café*. To each his café. This quest, to find at least one special café for everyone, as opposed to fifty cafés for anyone, lured me back to Paris sixteen times during the last four years, for stays of from one week to seven months long.

The fruits of my fixations encompass legendary haunts like Hemingway's Aux Deux Magots and Brasserie Lipp and Sartre and de Beauvoir's Café de Flore in St-Germain-des-Prés and neighborhood treasures—Au Roi du Café, Le Petit Château d'Eau, Aux Petits Joueurs—familiar mostly to locals. The compilation extends from the old bohemian quarters of Montparnasse and Montmartre to the new ones centered around Belleville and Oberkampf, from the youthful casualness of Dame Tartine to the long-standing perfectionism of Pétrissans. You will encounter a glitzy, retro *moderne* classic like Brasserie Lutétia in the heart of the Left Bank, while uncovering a new, atypical spot like the Web Bar, an Internet café/artspace with good tarts and chocolate cake, in the Marais. There is alluring Café de l'Industrie, a colonial, decadent, Art Deco temple for the Bastille intelligentsia, as well as Les Fontaines, a grotesque, yellow-neon

remnant of 1970s style with bistro foods and wines of timeless taste.

Discussion of these cafés, as well as the attitudes, postures, moods, conversations, relationships, and eating and drinking habits found within, invariably illuminates cultural differences between the French and Americans. The purpose here is to celebrate these differences—not to reconcile them—and to defend them against their common foes. The Parisian café is at the heart of a rich culture threatened, like many of our own regional treasures, by the homogenizing influx of fast-food joints, shopping malls, video games, the Internet, sixty-hour work weeks, and the global marketplace. Reading, cooking, and eating your way through this book should give you a full appreciation of what makes this institution so worth preserving.

More significantly, you should be prepared to choose a regular Parisian café to call your own. Two, ten, or fifty would be even better!

How to use this book: This book is organized for the convenience of the home cook. Recipes are grouped in the order of a meal: first appetizers, then side dishes and main courses, and finally desserts. One recipe from each of the fifty featured cafés (see map and café listings on page viii) is preceded by a companion essay that depicts the characters and characteristics that make that particular place special. If a café has more than one recipe, the names and page numbers for those recipes are listed at the end of the essay. To find what's written about a specific café, search the index.

Appetizers

Clown Bar

114, rue Amelot
Tel: 01 43 55 87 35
Métro: Filles du Calvaire

Joe Vitte wants it understood he's nothing like the frolicking clowns depicted in the wondrous strip of ceramic tiles that adorn his breathtakingly restored café beside the Cirque d'Hiver (winter circus) theater. Never mind doing cartwheels or juggling wine bottles, he won't go so far as to put on a happy face for his wide-eyed audience. "We're not the smiling type," he warns potential and, to my mind, perfectly respectable paying customers. "We scowl when we feel like it." At times, a scowl is only the half of it.

With straggly grayish hair hanging down both sides of his volatile visage, the rugged barman looks the part of a cantankerous circus performer stripped of his makeup and make-believe. His is a fitting profile for a 1919 offstage refuge that doubled for decades as a global employment agency for clowns passing through Paris. In 1988, Vitte, then an antiques dealer in the hunt for an old bistro, took over and polished up the abandoned institution, expanded the narrow space into the adjacent concierge's compartment, added a kitchen and cooked foods, and installed a custom-made zinc bar, bistro chairs and tables, and an ever-growing collection of circus lights, big-top posters, and clown art and memorabilia. Positioned, both geographically and temperamentally, between the affluent charm of the Marais quarter and raucous nightlife of Oberkampf and the Bastille, the quaint Clown Bar, or, if you prefer, Frown Bar, inhabits an easy-going middle ground on the contemporary Right Bank scene.

It is not, I am glad to report, the museum that might have been. Though he loves to show off his place to curious first-timers, especially Americans (he has trouble with British-accented English), and encourages parents to bring in their kids for lunch, Vitte desires above all a low-priced rendezvous of habitués that preserves bistro traditions as well as it does circus relics. Terrines, either of pork or of herring, are served in their entirety and *à volonté*—as much as you like. Humble classics like *oeufs en meurette* (poached eggs in red wine), *moules* (mussels) *rémoulade*, and *onglet* (flank steak) are approached with the utmost seriousness. New finds in *petits* (or unheralded) wines, notably from the Loire Valley, the Rhône Valley, and Beaujolais, are waiting to be discovered every month. The coffee dessert sampler, with a java-flavored pastry, mousse, ice cream, and *biscuit*, is an ensemble of sweet gestures from a host whose sincerely felt affection for his loyal following, including clowns from the Québec troupe Cirque de Soleil, is not always so apparent.

One evening shortly before closing, I found myself squeezed between an enraged Vitte and the obnoxious wine "connoisseur" he was trying to pummel. As the scuffle spun out onto the sidewalk, I was faced with this dilemma: Should I defend my counterpart, who, though no pal of mine, was somehow allied with my bistro buddies, or should I protect the touchy guy who controls access to this cherished pearl of a café? Suffice it to say, Vitte's unsmiling face did not suffer so much as a scratch.

MUSSELS AND ZUCCHINI SALAD WITH SPICY MAYONNAISE

MOULES RÉMOULADE

A most basic and economical seafood salad, mussels *rémoulade* is prepared by first steaming the bivalves in white wine, shallots, and herbs, as you would for classic mussels *à la marinière*. So as not to be wasteful, it is suggested that glasses of the unused wine left in the bottle—preferably Muscadet, the ideal accompaniment—be served with the salad.

1. Melt the butter in a large pot over medium-high heat. Add the shallots and cook until translucent, 2 to 3 minutes.

2. Add the wine, bay leaf, parsley, thyme, mussels, salt, and pepper, cover the pot, and steam the mussels, shaking the pot occasionally, until the shells open, 6 to 9 minutes. Remove the mussels with a slotted spoon, and let cool.

3. Put the mayonnaise in a large bowl and season with the lemon juice and a little Tabasco. Remove the mussels from their shells. Add the shelled mussels and zucchini sticks to the mayonnaise, mix well, and refrigerate.

4. To serve, garnish with the carrot slices and chives.

MAKES 4 SERVINGS

PREPARATION TIME:
15 MINUTES

COOKING TIME: 12 MINUTES

2 tablespoons unsalted butter

3 shallots, chopped

¾ cup dry white wine (such as Muscadet)

1 bay leaf

¼ cup chopped fresh parsley

3 to 4 sprigs fresh thyme

4 pounds mussels, cleaned

Salt and freshly ground black pepper

½ cup mayonnaise (page 6)

1 teaspoon fresh lemon juice

A dash of Tabasco sauce

4 medium zucchini, cut into thin 4-inch sticks

½ carrot, peeled and thinly sliced

2 tablespoons chopped chives

POACHED EGGS IN ASPIC

Oeufs en Gelée

Start thinking about how lovely your poached eggs are going to look, encased in domes of cognac-scented aspic, at the moment you begin filling the ramekins with ham and tarragon leaves. What you turn out will only be as elegant as the decorative manner in which you assemble it. For an excellent consommé, search no further than the recipe for *pot-au-feu* (page 97). Consider also poaching an extra egg in case one breaks.

1. In a medium saucepan over medium-low heat, heat all but ¼ cup of the stock to a simmer. Season well with salt and pepper (it should be highly seasoned). Add the cognac.

2. In a small saucepan, soften the gelatin in the remaining ¼ cup of cold stock. Place over a low heat and melt for about 1 minute. Add to the remaining hot stock and mix well. Remove from the heat.

3. In a pot over medium-high heat, bring the water to a simmer. Add the vinegar. Break in the eggs and poach for 3 minutes. Delicately remove the eggs with a slotted spoon and place on paper towels. Trim the whites to form even circles.

4. Arrange a few ham strips and 2 tarragon leaves on the bottoms of 6 ramekins. Pour a thin layer of aspic over the top of the ham and tarragon. Refrigerate for 10 to 15 minutes, until the aspic has set.

5. Delicately place 1 egg in each ramekin. Surround each egg with ham strips. Fill the ramekins with aspic. Chill for several hours.

6. To serve, run a knife around the inside edge of each ramekin. Dip the ramekins in hot water for a few seconds. Turn the egg and aspic out onto a serving dish.

MAKES 6 SERVINGS

PREPARATION TIME:
15 MINUTES

COOKING TIME: 15 MINUTES

2 cups beef consommé or
   veal stock

Salt and freshly ground
   black pepper

1 tablespoon cognac or
   Madeira wine

1 packet unflavored gelatin

1 quart water

3 tablespoons white wine
   vinegar

6 eggs

2 slices cooked ham, cut into
   thin strips

12 leaves fresh tarragon

4

Aux Tonneaux des Halles

28, rue Montorgueil
Tel: 01 42 33 36 19
Métro: Châtelet-Les Halles

Considering his domination of La Course des Garçons des Cafés, a grueling Paris mini-marathon open only to waiters burdened with a full service tray and their traditional black (slacks, heeled shoes, vest or jacket) and white (shirt and apron) uniform, you might expect six-time champion Patrick Fabre to push a low-fat, high-carbo regimen of pasta, whole grains, legumes, and broiled fish. But the road-running Auvergnat is big on cheeses, hams, pâtés, and, most of all, red meat. The only kind of beef he won't serve, or so says chef Pascal Christian, poking fun at a preference of some Americans, is "well done."

This endearing classic among the cafés and food shops of rue Montorgueil started out in 1907 as a depot for the *diables* (pushcarts) used at Les Halles, the legendary wholesale market (now a confusing shopping mall) that moved from here in the center of Paris to Rungis, near Orly Airport, in 1969. Later, Aux Tonneaux ("to the barrels") became one of the many nocturnal bistros serving early-morning *pot-au-feu, jarret de porc* (pig's knuckles), and *boeuf bourguignon* to food buyers and purveyors. Quite a few of their faces were captured in the mural that covers the rear wall. Old photos, an antique cash register, and vintage cubicles marked TOILETTE, TÉLÉPHONE, and OFFICE (the kitchen) also recall Les Halles' glorious past, while the cozy terrace and congenial staff—Martine and Christophe in the morning, Thierry and Jérôme in the afternoon—engage a relaxed, diverse clientele. More women have certainly visited the premises during the past twenty years than in the prior seventy.

Fabre cannot, however, attribute his racing laurels solely to Aux Tonneaux's fine rib steak *Bordelaise,* duck *rillettes* (preserved minced meat spread) from the Lot region, copious charcuterie plates, raspberry crumble, choice—and cholesterol-reducing—red wines, or even the honest *oeuf* (hard-boiled egg) *mayonnaise.* His family's eleven first-place finishes (five for his brother Marc), halted only by the "Fabre rule"—three wins and you're out—were facilitated by light-weight, black-leather moccasins stripped of their insoles and fitted with specially designed orthotics. *C'est les chaussures—* it's the shoes.

HARD-BOILED EGGS AND MAYONNAISE

Oeufs Mayonnaise

Now that many French kitchens are using store-bought mayonnaise from a jar (*quel travestissement!*), the simple pleasure of this bistro classic, when made with true, homemade mayo, is greater than ever. As humble a cold appetizer as it is, oeufs mayonnaise ought not be snubbed. I've met bistro connoisseurs of considerable financial and gustatory means who order the dish every day. Mayonnaise prepared in advance should be kept in a tight-lidded jar and stored in the refrigerator.

1. Thirty minutes in advance, take out the ingredients for the mayonnaise from the refrigerator and bring them to room temperature.

2. Put the beaten yolks, mustard, salt, and pepper in a round-bottomed mixing bowl, always resting it on a flat surface, and whisk until blended.

3. Add a dash of oil and beat well until the mixture begins to emulsify. Add the rest of the oil, drop by drop, continuously beating the mixture with a whisk until it becomes firm and very thick.

4. Add the vinegar, and more salt and pepper to taste. Set aside.

5. Delicately lower the eggs into a pot of boiling water and simmer for 10 to 12 minutes.

6. Plunge the eggs in cold water for 2 to 3 minutes. Peel off the shells and halve the boiled eggs.

7. To serve, place 3 halves of hard-boiled egg on each plate, spoon the mayonnaise over the eggs or to the side, and garnish with salad greens.

MAKES 4 SERVINGS

PREPARATION TIME:
10 MINUTES

COOKING TIME:
10 TO 12 MINUTES

FOR THE MAYONNAISE
(1 CUP)

2 egg yolks, beaten

1 teaspoon Dijon mustard

*Salt and freshly ground
    black pepper*

*1 cup fresh vegetable oil
    (preferably soybean,
    sunflower, or olive)*

*1 to 2 teaspoons white wine
    vinegar*

TO CONTINUE

6 eggs

Lettuce or salad greens

CELERY ROOT SALAD
WITH SPICY MAYONNAISE

Celeri Rémoulade

Some recipes for this elemental bistro appetizer call for you to soften the celery root by blanching it in boiling water, assuming that "softer" is in itself a desirable result. But Pétrissans and other members of the al dente school of *celeri rémoulade* rightly insist that it be as crunchy as possible. This is accomplished by using raw celery root, not shredding it too finely (it should be cut at least as wide as linguine and never so narrow as angel hair), and not combining it with the mayo until the last moment. (Note: If you peel and shred the celery root a couple of hours in advance, it must be tossed with a teaspoon of lemon juice before being stored in the refrigerator to prevent discoloration.)

1. Peel the celery root until all the surfaces are evenly white and unblemished. Either shred the celery root using the large holes of a grater or cut with a knife into matchsticks. Transfer to a large serving bowl.

2. In a mixing bowl, combine the mayonnaise, Tabasco, Worcestershire sauce, and Dijon mustard and mix well. Taste and correct the seasoning, adding salt and pepper and perhaps more Tabasco.

3. Immediately before serving, add the mayonnaise to the celery root and mix well.

MAKES 6 SERVINGS

PREPARATION TIME:
10 MINUTES

1 pound celery root

*1 cup mayonnaise
(page 6)*

½ teaspoon Tabasco

*1 teaspoon Worcestershire
sauce*

*1 teaspoon strong Dijon
mustard*

*Salt and freshly ground
black pepper*

CAFÉ DE LA PAIX

12, BOULEVARD DES CAPUCINES
TEL: 01 42 68 12 13
MÉTRO: OPÉRA

Zola, Maupassant, and Massenet were habitués. Caruso drew caricatures on the napkins. Legendary master chefs—Ninon, Escoffier, Debretagne, Vignon, Duglère—ruled the kitchen. And at least as many great romantic dramas were played out on the long café terrace as there were sung in arias on the stage of its magnificent place de l'Opéra neighbor, the Palais Garnier.

Nevertheless, Parisians who have not set foot in Café de la Paix—and even a couple of employees who must do so every day—identify the world-famous sidewalk café as the tourist trap where shutter-happy Japanese aim their viewfinders at sentimentalists grasping for the lost elegance of the *grands boulevards*. Remarks about its nostalgic habitués are a tradition nearly as old as the café itself. In the 1875 volume *Les Cafés Politiques et Littéraires de Paris*, author Arthur Lepage called it "the favorite rendezvous of imperialists nostalgic for the Second Empire." A cynic might say that still holds true.

But the ridicule, aside from being condescending toward the French provincials, foreigners, and, yes, fellow Parisians who adore the café's expansive view, overlooks an exciting development. Christian Le Squer, the gifted young chef who has earned two Michelin stars at the Restaurant Opéra, has taken charge of the menus in the café's brasserie. The café terrace, the interior brasserie, and the deluxe Restaurant Opéra are all part of the Grand Hôtel Inter-Continental. At the acclaimed restaurants Lucas Carton, Taillevent, and the Hôtel Ritz's Espadon, Le Squer helped maintain hard-won reputations. Now it's his responsibility to reverse one.

"The power that our name has is *impressionnant*," says the good-natured Le Squer, amused by the constant ribbing he gets from friends and colleagues. "They don't think of it as a restaurant. It will take three years to overcome the tourist image."

I might not wait that long. Le Squer's seasonal, three-course, 169-franc (about $28) lunch menu is a very good value and, for a café that asks 26 francs—roughly $4.35!—for a cup of espresso, something of a phenomenon. It has successfully showcased such contemporary, foreign-influenced French cuisine as red-pepper *quenelles* (fish mousse cakes) in tomato gazpacho, *acras de morue* (salt cod fritters) wrapped in the Middle Eastern pastry *kadaifi*, a *Tatin* of blood sausage and apples, and pan-fried veal flank with onion marmalade and Parmesan risotto. Time will tell if Le Squer's kitchen staff can maintain this fussy a program. As for the pampering waitresses of special comfort to the bankers who lunch alone, I have no reservations. These women are fabulous.

The café's handsomely restored dining area, with its Corinthian columns, golden moldings, and Italianate ceilings, envelopes you in the flamboyance of the Second Empire. It's enough to make you a nostalgic imperialist if you are not one already.

SALT COD CROQUETTES

ACRAS DE MORUE

Christian Le Squer prepares these delectable *acras* in a batter of *kadaifi,* a Middle Eastern dough that French chefs use to give their fried delicacies a crisp, shredded-wheat-like coating. Since *kadaifi* is found only in select Greek, Turkish, and Middle Eastern markets, you may have to use shredded filo or bread crumbs for dredging or proceed without any batter at all. A specialty of the French West Indies, *acras* may be served as an appetizer or as an hors d'oeuvre. Note that the salt cod must be soaked at least 24 hours in advance.

1. Soak the salt cod in several changes of cold water for 24 to 48 hours.

2. In a small bowl, combine the garlic and olive oil. Set aside.

3. Cook the potatoes in a pot of unsalted boiling water for 20 to 30 minutes, or until thoroughly cooked. Drain and set aside.

4. Meanwhile, combine the milk, water, bay leaf, and thyme. Add the salt cod. Bring to a boil, cover, and simmer over low heat for 10 minutes.

5. Drain the cod, remove and discard the bones and skin, and flake the fish with a fork. Process the fish in a food processor.

6. Mash the potatoes and stir the fish into them.

7. Bring the cream to a boil, and whisk little by little into the mashed potatoes.

8. Heat the olive oil and garlic over medium heat for 1 minute. Strain through a fine sieve and whisk into the mashed potatoes.

MAKES 6 SERVINGS

PREPARATION TIME (AFTER SOAKING THE COD 24 TO 48 HOURS): 25 MINUTES

COOKING TIME: 40 MINUTES

1 pound 4 ounces salt cod

4 cloves garlic, crushed

7 tablespoons olive oil

3 medium potatoes, peeled

2 cups milk

2 cups water

1 bay leaf

1 branch fresh thyme

7 tablespoons heavy cream

½ to ¾ teaspoon cayenne pepper (optional)

Salt and freshly ground black pepper

2 eggs

1 package kadaifi *(or substitute shredded filo or 1 cup bread crumbs)*

Vegetable oil for deep-frying

Lemons

Spicy tartar sauce (optional)

continued

9. Season the potatoes with the cayenne pepper and salt and black pepper to taste. When cool, form into small balls.

10. Beat the eggs in a small bowl and season with salt and pepper. Working 1 ball at a time, coat the *acras*. Dunk an *acra* ball in the egg and shake off any excess liquid. Tear off a clump of *kadaifi* (or shredded filo), loosen a little by gently pulling the strands with both hands, and wrap the dough around the ball. (If using bread crumbs, simply roll the balls gently in the bread crumbs.) Repeat until all the balls are wrapped. Then wet your hands and smooth over the *acra* balls between your palms so that the *kadaifi* strands lie flat.

11. Heat the deep-frying oil in a deep-fat fryer or heavy skillet (about 3 inches) until a drop of water sizzles when added, about 375°F. Drop the *acras* into the hot oil and deep-fry for 3 to 5 minutes. When they are puffed and brown, remove and drain on paper towels.

12. Serve with lemon or spicy tartar sauce.

BRASSERIE BALZAR

49, RUE DES ÉCOLES

TEL: 01 43 54 13 67

MÉTRO: CLUNY-SORBONNE, ST-MICHEL

Balzar's stature as the brasserie of Latin Quarter intellectuals does not date back to its opening by Amédée Balzar in 1897 or even to its purchase and subsequent Art Deco makeover by the great Marcellin Cazes of Brasserie Lipp in 1931. The institution still known as the second Lipp long after the Cazes family's 1961 retreat did not truly become a Left Bank legend until after its globe lights, porcelain vases, and tilted-down mirrors were somehow spared amid the student riots in May of 1968. The escape was viewed as an act of divine or collegiate intervention by journalists, editors, and academics, who immediately seized the café left standing as their rendezvous.

Aside from its proximity to boulevard St-Michel and the Sorbonne, what distinguishes Balzar among Paris's great literary brasseries is its intimate scale. Each moleskin banquette and classic bistro chair affords its occupant a position of importance. Two elderly vacationers from Michigan seated next to a French rap star at table 36, for a time the province of Simone de Beauvoir and Jean-Paul Sartre, is hardly an unusual juxtaposition in a small, open dining room with no Siberias or quarantines. Instead of merely tolerating guests from across the Atlantic, current owner Jean-Pierre Egurreguy goes so far as to boast about a sizable clientele consisting solely of, by his account, American Francophiles who live near the ocean.

"The Americans who come here are not from Texas and Mississippi," he says, betraying the characteristically Parisian arrogance obscured by Balzar's openness. "They're from the coasts. They're sophisticated artists, models, students, professors, and families who know France, who love France."

Those who know and love Balzar realize you don't have to be making history, much less studying, teaching, or editing it, to fit in with the lunch crowd. But it is helpful to dress and act the part. That necessitates expressions of ennui toward anyone famous who walks through the door, with exceptions made only for internationally known playwrights who are also the presidents of their countries. When Vaclav Havel came in for lunch on March 4, 1990, just three months after his election, Balzar gave the teary-eyed Czech leader a standing ovation.

Did Pierre Sauvet, Balzar's chef for the past quarter-century, prepare anything particularly imaginative or remarkable for President Havel? I sincerely doubt it. But his midday meal was almost certainly, as the French like to say, *correct*, by which they mean it respected custom. It was genuine. It was honest. And while a deluxe restaurant doing mashed potatoes and other comfort foods might interpret *"correct"* as a polite putdown, a traditional brasserie—even one as illustrious as Balzar—should view it as an accolade. Unlike young hot-shot chefs who try to reinvent the hard-boiled egg, Sauvet understands there isn't much he can—or should—do to improve *oeufs mayonnaise,*

celery root *rémoulade*, leeks vinaigrette, *soupe à l'oignon gratinée*, *sole meunière*, steak tartare, roast leg of lamb with white and green beans, profiteroles, or *poire belle Hélène* (poached pear with ice cream and chocolate sauce).

During my first months in Paris, I would pass by Balzar en route to the revival movie houses on rue Champollion, spot the odd open table on its single-row terrace, and flirt with but never follow through on the idea of changing my plans for the evening. Only after adding these nondecisions to a growing pile of maddening missed opportunities did I begin to see that open table, especially when there were attractive women seated on either side, as part of my destiny. Thereafter, I would without hesitation enter Balzar and take possession of my fate, as the intellectuals did in 1968.

BRASSERIE BALZAR: Onion Soup Gratinée *(page 13)*, Roast Leg of Lamb with Flageolet Beans *(page 75)*, Chocolate Profiteroles *(page 156)*

ONION SOUP GRATINÉE

SOUPE À L'OIGNON GRATINÉE

A single word, *gratinée,* is sufficient to order French onion soup. This version, made with water and white wine, is light enough so as not to completely rule out a meaty main course to follow. You may substitute a beef or chicken stock if you want to make the soup a meal.

1. Preheat the oven to 325°F.

2. Melt the butter in a large saucepan over medium heat, add the onions, and cook, stirring, until golden color sets in, 8 to 10 minutes. Add the flour and stir with the onions for 3 minutes.

3. Add the water, white wine, and bouquet garni and simmer for 30 minutes. Remove the bouquet garni, add salt and pepper to taste, and then pour the soup into 4 oven-proof bowls.

4. Dunk the rounds of toast into each bowl of soup and sprinkle liberally with the shredded Gruyère.

5. Bake in the oven for 15 minutes, then set under a hot broiler to brown the top.

MAKES 4 SERVINGS

PREPARATION TIME:
10 MINUTES

COOKING TIME: 1 HOUR

3 tablespoons unsalted
 butter

1½ pounds onions, thinly
 sliced

2 tablespoons flour

1 quart water

1 cup dry white wine
 (such as Mâcon)

1 bouquet garni (thyme,
 parsley, bay leaf)

Salt and freshly ground
 black pepper

1 baguette, sliced into thin
 rounds and toasted

½ pound Gruyère or Swiss
 cheese, shredded

13

The second half of the nineteenth century was a period of monumental change in Paris, giving rise to the Sacré-Coeur Basilica, the Opéra, the Sorbonne, the Eiffel Tower, and the café-bistro of the modern era. While cafés of one sort or another have flourished since the opening in 1686 of Procope, a Left Bank literary landmark that's now a restaurant, most of today's best-known cafés trace their origins some two hundred years later to the workers who migrated to Paris from the rural region of Auvergne in south-central France.

The Auvergnats claimed the back-breaking jobs Parisians wouldn't do. Many worked as water carriers, balancing two large buckets of water on a yoke over their shoulders and climbing six flights in Paris apartment houses that lacked modern plumbing. During the winter, when people used for washing hardly more water than they drank, the men supplemented their income by hauling three sources of heat: coal, wood, and wine. They were affectionately known as *charbougnats* (a corruption of *charbonnier*—"coal seller") or, more simply, *bougnats*.

Soon they were serving a plat du jour at their small depots clustered near the Bastille, which became known as *bistros*. People congregated around the *comptoir* (bar) for warmth and refreshment, either from liquid or people contact. As these *salons de la démocratie* grew, the *bougnats* summoned their relatives from back home or placed help-wanted ads in the weekly newspaper founded in 1882, *L'Auvergnat de Paris*.

These displaced provincials rarely took vacations or participated in cultural activities.

Nevertheless, their dominance of the expanding café trade extended to the Left Bank's legendary literary haunts. The "Three Musketeers of St-Germain-des-Prés"—the Flore's Paul Boubal, Lipp's Marcellin Cazes, and the Deux Magots' Mathivat family—were all Auvergnats. Ernest Fraux, co-founder of Montparnasse's La Coupole, hailed from Aveyron, the area of Auvergne that seems to breed bistro legends.

Their control extended to the wholesale side, with the Tafanel and Bertrand families controlling beer distribution and the Richards supplying much of the wine and coffee. Lending seed money to *bougnats*, these families constituted the café mafia, a term its members accept, to a point. "We're the good part of the mafia," says Anne Richard-Bellanger, granddaughter of the founder of Vins Richard and Cafés Richard.

Despite the diminishing influence of these families and their countrymen, several of the city's trendiest cafés were opened by a new wave of proprietors who trace their roots to Aveyron, among them Gilbert Costes of Le Café Marly and Didier Alaux of Pause Café. Maybe there really is something in the Auvergne soil that raises able Parisian *cafetiers* (café operators). Still, the overriding factor may have more to do with a credit bias. Banks rarely lend unproven entrepreneurs money for café startups, and the family-run companies that do may submit candidates to an oral application consisting of two questions: (1) Are you married? (2) Where are you from? The answers that may lead to a handshake agreement are *"oui"* and *"Auvergne."*

Brasserie de l'Île St-Louis

55, quai de Bourbon
Tel: 01 48 87 44 13
Métro: Pont-Marie

The south-facing chairs on the terrace outside Brasserie de l'Île St-Louis constitute one of the most inviting places in Paris for summer *flâneurs* to park their bottoms. The red awning beckons strollers crossing from Île de la Cité to Île St-Louis and the historic sight of the first café in Paris to carry the island's famous ice creams. A single scoop of Berthillon's incomparable vanilla melting over a warm wedge of the brasserie's *tarte Tatin* is a thrill of Notre Dame proportions.

Nevertheless, the small-village charms of Île St-Louis and the warmth of a café that's hung around since 1870 are best felt in the dead of winter. Firstly, the robust cooking for which this and other Alsatian brasseries are adored—and sometimes feared—is not suitable for summer wear. Such classics as *choucroute garni* (sauerkraut plated here with ham, lard, and pork loin) and *jarret de porc* (pig's knuckles) are the heavy woolens of the French kitchen wardrobe. Even the lighter fish *choucroute,* made with smoked haddock (finnan haddie), will weigh you down. Second, this brasserie takes on the home-away-from-home comfort of an old tavern only when Paris shuts itself indoors. By early autumn, you get the impression that owner Michele Kappe is counting time as well as money from her cashier's post, eagerly awaiting the first cold front to pass over the Seine.

"Summer is very agreeable and we are valued for our terrace," says Madame Kappe, whose parents purchased the business in 1953, *"mais"*—always heed what the French say after, and not before, their word for *but*—"winter is more convivial. The island is deserted. Inside it's noisy. It's like a pub, an old bistro."

Her preference for the season when tourists are least visible should in no way be interpreted as an antiforeign sentiment. Quite the contrary. Though the brasserie's food and grammar are unmistakably French, Kappe and her long-standing staff's genuine fondness for Anglophones has made the brasserie a popular drinking haunt for English-speaking visitors and expats. They really like us. At least our better half.

"Américaines are adorable," Gino the waiter declares, and I beam, not comprehending that he has flattered only the female form of my nationality. *"Mais* not *américains,"* he adds, remarking on the male form. Am I insulted? Hardly. The banter across the communal tables and under the beer-barreled chandeliers is what brings people back, Australian students and French prime ministers alike. Gino and barman Yvan have over sixty-five years of combined experience teasing the people they serve. Should either man ride you too far, you may wish to comment on his advancing age by asking what apparatus he personally used to brew coffee before the Paris Express copper-plated coffee maker was installed behind the bar. The machine, said to be the oldest still-functioning one of its kind in Paris, was put in place in 1913.

BRASSERIE DE L'ÎLE ST-LOUIS: Onion Tart *(page 16)*, Fish Choucroute *(page 128)*

ONION TART

TARTE À L'OIGNON

Serve a small slice of this classic Alsatian tart as an appetizer or a larger slice, along with a salad, as a main course.

1. Preheat the oven to 450°F.

2. In a large pot, bring the water to a boil, add the onions, and cook for 6 minutes. Drain.

3. Put the onions, crème fraîche, eggs, herbs, and salt and pepper in a large bowl and mix well.

4. Use the butter to grease a 9-inch tart pan. With a rolling pin, roll out the pastry dough to a ⅛-inch thickness. Line the tart pan with the rolled dough.

5. Pour the onion mixture into the tart and top evenly with diced bacon.

6. Place the tart on a baking sheet and bake for 30 to 40 minutes, until golden brown.

MAKES 6 SERVINGS AS APPETIZER; 4 SERVINGS AS MAIN COURSE

PREPARATION TIME: 10 MINUTES (PLUS 1 HOUR 10 MINUTES FOR MAKING THE DOUGH)

COOKING TIME: 55 MINUTES

1 quart water

1½ pounds onions, peeled and sliced

3 tablespoons crème fraîche (recipe follows), or sour cream

2 eggs, beaten

1 teaspoon herbes de Provence

Salt and freshly ground black pepper

1 recipe Pie Pastry (page 146)

1 tablespoon unsalted butter

2 strips bacon, diced

A beauty cream from the French dairy case that enhances the pluses and conceals the minuses of various food preparations, crème fraîche consists of heavy cream thickened to the consistency of sour cream by lactic bacteria. (At home, buttermilk is used to supply the fermenting agents.) Its sharp flavor, more tangy than it is sour, and creaminess enrich cooked vegetables, sauces, soups, and, when used as a cool dessert topping, tarts, crumbles, fruit compotes, mousses, and cakes.

1. Heat the heavy cream in a saucepan over low heat until warm; pour into a jar. Add the buttermilk, close the lid tightly, and shake well.

2. Let sit at room temperature until the cream thickens, at least 12 hours and not more than 24 hours. Store in the refrigerator.

Note: For subsequent batches, reserve a tablespoon of crème fraîche and use it instead of the buttermilk.

MAKES ABOUT 1 CUP

PREPARATION TIME:
5 MINUTES
(PLUS 12 TO 24 HOURS
TO FERMENT)

1 cup heavy cream

1 tablespoon buttermilk

LE CAFÉ MARLY

93, RUE DE RIVOLI
TEL: 01 49 26 06 60
MÉTRO: PALAIS-ROYAL

The café romantic can do the Left Bank rounds of Montparnasse and St-Germain-des-Prés, sit in chairs the behinds of Picasso, Hemingway, and Sartre once kept warm, and imagine himself one of them and one with them. But the nearest he may ever get to the exhilaration of that glorious past is in the glittery present of the Right Bank's Le Café Marly, which, though situated in a great museum, cannot be confused with one. It's a contemporary café-brasserie percolating with possibilities, a gathering of cultural, media, and political pacesetters—and pretenders—with room for an American neophyte eager to throw himself into their milieu. The relentless clacking of silver-

ware against plates, French chatter against multilingual repartee, and champagne flutes against each other is the unmistakable sound, then and now, of Paris coming together.

The new-generation Auvergnat looking after the encounter is Gilbert Costes, who builds his glamorous latter-day Lipps (Le Café Marly, Café Beaubourg, and Café de la Musique were all inspired by Brasserie Lipp) near museums, away from cars, and behind grand terraces. Marly's terrace is a long, vaulted gallery with canvas-covered chairs, banquettes, and stools overlooking the Louvre's Cour Napoléon and Pyramid. In early spring, its leisurely rapport with the museum's regal court hints at the elegant relationship the famous Café Florian has to Venice's Piazza San Marco. In July, its view is that of a veranda at a summer resort, Louvre Beach perhaps. Inside are two neoclassical rooms—one blue, one red, neither Siberia (though center tables 13 and 14 in the red room are the best to see from and be seen in)—lushly furnished with sensuous banquettes, velour chairs distinguished by the ringed brass handles on their backs, and the striking centerpiece, an octopus-like glass chandelier with cups and saucers balanced on the ends of its tentacles. Below the terrace is sunny court-level seating for beverage service only.

Marly is often misunderstood by newcomers of both foreign and domestic origin. Those expecting a conventional restaurant, understandable with main courses priced up to 150 francs (about $25), are disappointed to find themselves seated at small round café tables paired like figure eights for groups of four. Those envisioning a café may wonder why there's neither a *comptoir* (bar) to stand at nor the freedom to sit wherever they like. But the kitchen, supervised by Jacques Barbery, the eternal second-in-command to great chefs finally stepping up to general, tries to accommodate all appetites. The brasserie menu, marked by fast, simple preparation, is a mix of worldly, fashionable, capably done snack foods and indulgences (guacamole, gazpacho, basmati rice, tomato and buffalo mozzarella, couscous, Caesar salad) alongside more traditional meats and seafood. The *gâteau* of tomato and goat cheese with tapenade garnish, decadent puréed potatoes, and salmon fillet *unilatéral* (seared on the skin side only) are quite good, as is—though certain snobs and antisnob snobs may not care to hear it—the softly hand-packed, 90-franc (roughly $15) cheeseburger on a sesame seed brioche bun.

The cool reception and rigid service provided by Marly's staff often comes across as chilly arrogance. That perception is largely due to the punctilious operation put in place by Costes, coordinated by manager Bruno Garcia, and criticized by those who reject the protocol. When a maître d' gives a client the once-over, it's to determine if his is the prim posture of an individual who, once seated, wants his chair pushed in for him and his menu opened for him. More easygoing diners are allowed to do this for themselves, although they are admonished for daring to move someone else's chair. Transferring an empty stool from one terrace table to another is looked upon as a felony. With the café's five hundred seats carefully positioned—and attended to—for optimal order and efficiency, Marly's policy is to be fair but firm resolving disputes with clients.

One warm afternoon, a man in Rollerblades took a seat on the court-level terrace near the crowds outside the Pyramid, ordered a Perrier, and placed a 200-franc (about $35) note on his table. When the money vanished, the man complained first to the waiter and then, vehemently, to Garcia and threatened to call his lawyer. Garcia stood his ground, not aware of the Paris journalist sitting nearby and taking notes for an article supportive of his rationale that would be published in the daily *Le Parisien* the following day.

"My garçon had not touched the bill," Garcia explained to me from the site of the altercation. "I can't be held responsible for the wind."

Two days later, Garcia went for a stroll atop the Louvre's Richelieu wing and found a 200-franc note resting on the outer cornice some fifty meters over the café.

LE CAFÉ MARLY: Tomato and Goat Cheese Cake *(page 20)*, Decadent Mashed Potatoes *(page 41)*

TOMATO AND GOAT CHEESE CAKE

GÂTEAU AU TOMATES ET CHÈVRE

At Le Café Marly, this adorable mini cake with alternating layers of tomato confit and goat cheese is served on a small plate with a ribbon of cold tomato sauce, croutons, a basil leaf, and a teaspoon of tapenade. In addition to—or in place of—these garnishes, you may wish to add some fresh herbs to the goat cheese mixture. The cake can also be prepared as a terrine in a 1½-quart loaf pan and cut into slices while still cold.

1. Preheat the oven to 225°F.

2. In a baking dish, toss the quartered tomatoes with 2 tablespoons of the olive oil and a little salt. Bake in the oven for 1½ hours.

3. Meanwhile, soften the goat cheese to room temperature. In a bowl, combine the goat cheese with the *fromage blanc*, the remaining tablespoon olive oil, and the lemon juice and Tabasco, and mix well with a fork. Add salt and pepper to taste.

4. Cut or break the tomato sections into thin pieces and use ⅓ of them to fully cover the bottoms of 6 ramekins with a ¼-inch layer of tomato. Flatten with the back of a spoon if necessary.

5. Top the tomato with a ½-inch layer of the goat cheese mixture, making sure the surface is flat and even.

6. Top the goat cheese with another ¼-inch layer of tomato so that no white is showing. Top with a second layer of goat cheese, leaving just enough room for a final ¼-inch layer of tomato.

7. Top off the cakes with the remaining tomato and refrigerate for at least 4 hours or up to 5 days.

MAKES 6 INDIVIDUAL CAKES

PREPARATION TIME: 20 MINUTES (PLUS AT LEAST 4 HOURS REFRIGERATION)

COOKING TIME: 1 HOUR 30 MINUTES

5 or 6 tomatoes, quartered and seeds removed

3 tablespoons olive oil

Salt

1 pound fresh goat cheese

1 cup fromage blanc (see Note)

2 teaspoons fresh lemon juice

A dash of Tabasco sauce

Salt and freshly ground black pepper

½ cup plum tomato sauce (optional)

2 tablespoons tapenade (page 117; optional)

6 leaves fresh basil (optional)

1 baguette, thinly sliced and toasted

8. To serve, carefully run a knife around the edges of the ramekins to loosen the cakes. Unmold by turning them over onto individual plates. Garnish, if desired, with a swirl of tomato sauce, a teaspoon of tapenade, and a basil leaf. Serve with toasted baguette slices.

Note: *Fromage blanc* is a soft, creamy cheese made by draining thick curd of its whey. It's a staple of the French dairy case, comes in a variety of fat contents (0%, 3%, 6%, etc.), and is often consumed with fruit or sugar and cream. It is also used like a yogurt in sauces, marinades, and hors d'oeuvres. Cottage cheese, which may be its closest American counterpart, is blander, not as creamy, a tad sweeter, and doesn't have the same acidy character. If you are unable to find American-made *fromage blanc* (Vermont Butter & Cheese Company is one brand) at a local gourmet market, I've found the most suitable substitute to be yogurt cheese.

To prepare yogurt cheese at home: Spoon plain lowfat yogurt into a coffee filter, set over a bowl, cover, place in the refrigerator, and let drain 5 to 6 hours but not longer. One pound yogurt will yield 1 cup yogurt cheese.

STUFFED ARTICHOKES WITH RATATOUILLE NIÇOISE

FONDS D'ARTICHAUTS RATATOUILLE NIÇOISE

1. Preheat the oven to 400°F.

2. Break the stems off the base of the artichokes, remove the small bottom leaves, and, using scissors, clip off the prickly points of the remaining leaves. Wash the artichokes well in a large pot of water containing 1 tablespoon of vinegar per quart of water, then drain.

3. Cook the artichokes in a large pot of boiling salted water for 45 minutes, and drain. When cool enough to handle, remove the leaves (they may be served separately with the vinaigrette) and carefully carve away the chokes from the artichoke hearts.

4. Meanwhile, heat 1 tablespoon of the olive oil in a saucepan over medium heat and cook the onion and pepper until lightly brown, about 10 minutes. Add the tomatoes and reduce the heat to low.

5. In a separate saucepan, heat 1 tablespoon olive oil over medium-high heat, and cook the zucchini until softened, about 5 minutes. Repeat with the eggplant. Drain both from their liquid and add to the tomato, onion, and pepper mixture. Add the garlic and bouquet garni, season with salt and pepper, and simmer over low heat for 15 minutes. Remove the bouquet garni.

6. Place the artichoke hearts in a buttered baking dish, fill each with ratatouille, and cook in the oven for 10 minutes. Drizzle with vinaigrette and serve immediately.

Note: *To peel tomatoes,* plunge in boiling water for 30 seconds to 1 minute, drain, and peel. *To peel a red pepper,* pierce it with a fork and turn it directly over a gas flame until the skin is blistered and blackened on all sides. Place the pepper in a paper bag and steam for 5 minutes. Rub off the skin with a paper towel.

MAKES 6 SERVINGS

PREPARATION TIME:
25 MINUTES

COOKING TIME: 1 HOUR

6 large artichokes

White wine vinegar

3 tablespoons olive oil

1 medium onion, chopped

1 red pepper, peeled, seeds removed, and cut into cubes (see Note)

2 medium tomatoes, peeled and chopped (see Note)

¼ pound zucchini, cut into cubes

¼ pound eggplant, cut into cubes

1 clove garlic, minced

1 bouquet garni (bay leaf, thyme, parsley)

Salt and freshly ground black pepper

Butter for greasing baking dish

½ cup vinaigrette (page 42)

When fashions change from generation to generation rather than season to season, the introduction of a radically different style is apt to arouse both vehement resistance and overzealous acceptance. Paris café society has thus been sharply divided in its response to the *bûchette*, the century's boldest new design in sugar packaging.

The slender-cut *bûchette* (small log) is a paper tube about 4 inches in length and ½ inch in diameter that contains two teaspoons of granulated sugar. Its late arrival in the city's cafés is yet another stunning symptom of Paris's eroding reputation as the fashion capital of the world. The sugar *bûchette* was launched more than a decade ago in Tokyo and premiered in Milan at least three years before its Left Bank debut during the winter of 1995.

Deeply ingrained loyalties may explain the delay. In the global marketplace, Northern France remains among the last bastions of sugar cubes. The number of them an individual takes in his daily cup(s) is an essential part of his personal identity. The quick dunking of a cube in a coffee or liqueur, producing a sugar candy referred to as a *canard*, is a time-honored, if not very elegant, ritual within the café experience. Less savory still is the recycling habit of thrifty café owners, who prefer cubes to granulated packets because their kitchens can make use of the ones left behind.

The region's enduring attachment to sugar cubism might be connected to the old custom of buying large chunks of hard sugar at the local market and breaking off smaller pieces as needed. Now that sugar comes prepackaged, Parisians may derive a visceral pleasure in reenacting that outdated custom by breaking apart a sugar cube into smaller pieces. Furthermore, the French can get anxious about measurements, especially those defined by spoonfuls (their flatware sets may contain spoons in five different sizes). Premeasured sugar cubes are a source of reassurance in an uncertain world.

Another advantage of sugar cubes is that the temperature of the coffee may be gauged by the speed at which they dissolve. If a cube dissolves too slowly, a practiced drinker will know to send the cup back without subjecting himself to the unpleasant experience of tasting the tepid brew.

The practical drawbacks to sugar cubes are threefold. First, although cubes allow for a precise sugar dosage, what's to be done when a quantity of, say, more than one cube but less than two is desired? Using your fingers to break apart a second cube into smaller pieces is a messy business. Alternatively, the act of removing that second cube from the cup before it is completely dissolved is, at best, problematic. It requires a level of concentration most of us can achieve only *after* we've had our caffeine fix. Second, the hard sugar cube breaks—and thus damages—the golden cream that floats sensually atop a coffee brewed under the high pressure of an espresso machine, as all the cups in Parisian cafés now are, whereas granulated sugar leaves the fragile mousse largely unharmed. Last, a sugar cube does not dissolve as easily in milk-added drinks like *café crème* (espresso and hot milk) and cappuccino.

The *bûchette* puts the delicacy and flexibility of granulated sugar in a groovy, user-friendly package. Once torn open at either end, its long narrow shape allows for greater control of sugar flow than the flat, squarish packets of sugar (and sugar substitutes) common in North America. Would-be coffee connoisseurs (true ones add no sugar at all) can sample a brew, assess its relative sweetness and bitterness, and then regulate exactly how much sugar they want to add to their cup.

Naturally, the practical merits of the *bûchette* may have little to do with its immense popularity in trendy cafés or its rejection in their old-fashioned counterparts. *La bûchette* is new; therefore it's hip. Sugar cubism is a long-standing Parisian institution.

"There isn't much variation in the sugar market so I'm not surprised the *bûchette* is very *à la mode*," noted a marketing spokesman for Eurosucre, the French sugar giant. "I believe there is a special cultural attachment to the whole pieces of sugar and they'll always exist. I can't say that yet about the *bûchette*."

CAFÉ CANNIBALE

93, RUE JEAN-PIERRE-TIMBAUD

TEL: 43 38 48 51

MÉTRO: COURONNES

English expatriate Sheridan Williams opened Café Cannibale during the winter of 1995 as a sanctuary for unchaperoned women. She desperately wanted a place where young women could come in alone and not be hounded by *dragueurs* (pick-up artists), unless, of course, they desired that kind of attention.

A favorable write-up in the June 11, 1995, issue of *Libération,* the left-leaning daily that informs culturally enlightened intellectuals, hailed Cannibale as that rare café that respects women. On June 12, Williams's "women's" café was packed with what appeared to be every *dragueur* in Paris.

"You can't change the French mentality," sighs Williams, who didn't help her cause any by choosing the name Cannibale.

Williams and her partner/boyfriend Tahar had far greater success establishing a popular hangout and reckless kitchen that feed off the ethnic diversity of the neighborhood. Belleville is a working-class area of dilapidated old apartment buildings and banal public housing inhabited by Arabs, Africans, Yugoslavs, Turks, Southeast Asians, Tunisian Jews, and northward-migrating bohemians priced out of art colonies in the Marais and the Bastille. The immediate area is largely populated by fundamentalist Arabs who, thanks to Tahar's Algerian roots, tolerate the midnight racket a whole lot better than the sleepless *Paris Match* journalist living above the café. He eventually moved out.

The prior proprietor served an Arab clientele, filled the space with slot machines, and obscured many of its original fixtures. Restoration-minded Williams was inclined first to strip down rather than dress up the walls surrounding the arched mirrors and fading stained-glass windows.

The eclectic playlist—only the high volume is a constant—incorporates Celtic, Arab, Breton, African, Brazilian, jazz, techno-pop, and reggae. For a while, Zsuzsanna Va'rhouyi, a young Hungarian accordionist, enchanted the Belleville mosaic on Sunday nights with Yiddish melodies while a world cuisine was improvised by two guitar-playing cooks: Brazilian Silvio Ricarti and Frenchman Christophe Barnier. The Ricarti I met was a lovable maniac bored by what he saw as the narrow scope of French cooking and the limited rotation of the usual café's plats du jour. "Everything's the same with them," he complains. "Even with the names—Véronique, Virginie, Valérie, Valentine . . . " He preferred to improvise piquant sauces, cold Peruvian-inspired seafood salads, Brazilian *feijoada* (black bean stew) and *acarajé* (black-eyed pea croquettes).

Ironically, the kitchen's real breakthrough in fusion cooking was accomplished by Barnier with his adaptations of the Tunisian delicacies known as *bricks*—filo-like sheets of flour pastry traditionally filled with egg, lamb or chicken, onion, and spices, then fried. Barnier purchased *bricks* at the nearby Arab markets and tried out all kinds of combos: ham and cheese, chili, couscous, potato and onions. His greatest success, a honey-dipped trio of cucumber, onion, and golden raisins, was one of the most oddly thrilling flavor coalitions I have ever encountered.

25

BRICKS WITH RAISINS, CUCUMBERS, AND ONIONS

BRICKS AUX RAISINS SECS, CONCOMBRES, ET OIGNONS

Tunisian *bricks* are round, paper-thin sheets of pastry traditionally filled with egg and Middle Eastern spices and then fried. A growing number of French chefs—and home cooks—are employing them in place of filo as a ready-to-use format for crisp pastries, savory and sweet. Le Café Marly fills its appetizer *bricks* with goat cheese. La Poule au Pot's *croustillant aux poires* is a dessert consisting of baked, pear-filled *bricks* served with hot chocolate sauce and fresh mint. Packages of *bricks* are available at groceries, street markets, and supermarkets throughout Paris, but nowhere in the U.S. You'll have to use sheets of filo cut into 8- to 12-inch rounds or squares or the spring roll wrappers (only use the ones without eggs) sold in Asian specialty markets.

1. Place the raisins in a bowl and add water to cover. (This keeps them soft and prevents them from puncturing the wrapper.)

2. Separate the spring roll wrappers and fill the center of each with small handfuls (1 to 2 tablespoons) of the cucumbers, onions, and, using a slotted spoon to drain, raisins. Season the fillings with salt and pepper and fold by lifting the bottom of the wrappers over the fillings, then the side flaps, and finally the tops.

3. Heat the vegetable oil in a skillet over medium heat.

4. Holding the folds in place, turn the bundles, and place them in the skillet, folded sides down. Cook until crisp and golden brown, about 1 minute, turn, and cook until the undersides are also golden brown. Remove, drain on paper towels, spoon a teaspoon or so of honey on top of each *brick,* and *serve* immediately.

MAKES 6 SERVINGS

PREPARATION TIME:
10 MINUTES

COOKING TIME: 5 MINUTES

1 cup raisins

*12 spring roll wrappers
(or substitute 1 package
filo dough)*

*2 cucumbers, peeled and
diced*

*2 medium onions, peeled
and diced*

*Salt and freshly ground
black pepper*

¼ cup vegetable oil

¼ cup honey

Brasserie Lutétia

23, rue de Sèvres
Tel: 45 44 38 10
Métro: Sèvres-Babylone

The mirrored pillar that obscures table 98 at the glitzy Brasserie Lutétia grants French movie star Jean-Paul Belmondo and other luminaries who request that corner banquette the illusion of privacy. But it didn't shield my cousin Philomène and me from the disapproving glances of the bourgeoisie. A twosome seated nearby, miffed to see *our* kind occupying table *quatre-vingt-dix-huit*, summoned night manager Patrick Massellucci, complained about the volume of our dialogue, and demanded a mid-appetizer move to another *arrondissement*. Massellucci responded with his one-word job description, *aplomb*.

"*Américains*," he sneered to the rapidly relocated couple. "You know how they are." Mission accomplished, he spun away and then floated back to our table to pardon what might have been perceived as a great indignity.

"Parisians," he sneered. "You know how they are."

Massellucci later noted that the unhappy couple was typical of the Lutétia's sizable bourgeois clientele. "They're never satisfied," he confided, "and yet they always come back." Even so, objecting to noisy chatter at the Lutétia is like complaining about bubbles in champagne. For *le tout* Paris knows that sitting removed from the brasserie's conversation-congested currents and floodlit sight lines is of no greater interest to the Queen of Spain than it is for the flabbergasted Spanish tourists seated across the aisle.

Although the deluxe Hôtel Lutétia and its reputation as a residence for scarcely starving artists date back to 1910, its brasserie is a relatively new addition. Formerly a rotisserie, it was retrofitted in 1974 by restaurant designer Slavik and fashion's Sonia Rykiel. Their Jazz Age–inspired room possesses all the icy enticement of a ruby-lipsticked smile followed by a bare, slender, yet very cold shoulder. Deco bar fixtures are finished in mirrors, stainless steel, polished chrome, and more mirrors.

Chef Philippe Renard's subterranean kitchen doubles as the cooking facility for the hotel's Michelin-one-starred restaurant, Le Paris. The quick-service brasserie menu has taught Renard a lesson mastered by too few of his peers. France's most ambitious young chefs often share with seven-year-old kids learning to paint the same artistic caveat: Their stuff is better if you stop them ten minutes before they think they're done. Otherwise, they are inclined to "paint over" whatever good they've already accomplished.

To simplify his seasonal menu, Renard showcases a single product for an entire month. If April is "lamb month," the daily specials will include at least three regional lamb dishes. Thus, a regular can return to the same corner banquette night after night (not unreasonable with a 180-franc—about $30—prix-fixe), order the same meat, and still experience a variety of cooking styles. The only missing ingredients are the two things the Lutétia habitué demands most and desires least: quiet and privacy.

BRASSERIE LUTÉTIA: Multicolored Melon Balls with Sauternes-Mint Sauce *(page 28)*, Golden Sea Scallops with Braised Leeks, Cream, and Fresh Herbs *(page 103)*, Veal Chop with Carmelized Carrots and Pearl Onions *(page 118)*, Chocolate Mousse *(page 170)*

MULTICOLORED MELON BALLS WITH SAUTERNES-MINT SAUCE

BILLES DE MELONS MULTICOLORES AU SAUTERNES ET À LA MENTHE

A beautiful, refreshing, sophisticated summer appetizer, dessert, or fruit cocktail that's simple and fun to do.

1. Scoop out the melon balls with a small scooper, removing as much of the melon as possible. Remove the seeds from the watermelon balls.

2. Pour yourself a small glass of Sauternes and combine the remainder with the honey, ginger, ½ the mint leaves (reserving the rest for the garnish), and lemon juice in a food processor or blender and mix well. Refrigerate the sauce for at least 1 hour.

3. Place the melon balls in 6 glass fruit cups.

4. Pour the Sauternes-mint sauce over the melon balls, top with almonds, and garnish with the remaining mint leaves.

MAKES 6 SERVINGS

PREPARATION TIME:
15 MINUTES (PLUS 1 HOUR
FOR CHILLING)

2 pounds watermelon, halved

1 honeydew, halved and pits removed

1 cantaloupe, halved and pits removed

1 bottle Sauternes (or substitute Muscatel or other sweet dessert wine)

1 tablespoon honey

1 ounce fresh ginger, peeled

1 bunch fresh mint

Juice of 1 lemon

½ cup sliced blanched almonds

VEGETABLE TERRINE WITH VINAIGRETTE

TERRINE DE LÉGUMES AU VINAIGRETTE

Polka-dotted slices of this vegetable terrine are a fresh and adorable summer alternative to heavy meat pâtés. You can layer the vegetables in any order and assortment, so long as you choose ones that hold their shape (broccoli and cauliflower do not generally work). The terrine may also be assembled in 6 separate ramekins, but you'll have to cut the vegetables into shorter pieces.

1. Bring a large pot of salted water to a boil. Add the carrot sticks, zucchini sticks, and turnip sticks and cook for 8 minutes. Drain, plunge the vegetables into ice water to stop the cooking and set in the color, and drain again.

2. Bring another pot of salted water to a boil. Add the green beans and cook for 10 minutes. Drain, plunge in ice water, and drain again.

3. Bring another pot of salted water to a boil. Add the green peas and cook for 3 minutes. Drain, plunge in ice water, and drain again.

4. Meanwhile, melt the butter in a saucepan over medium heat, add the shallot and herbs, and cook, stirring, until the shallot is translucent, 3 to 5 minutes. Pour in the sherry (or white wine) to deglaze the pan. Pour in the cream and simmer for 5 minutes.

5. Slowly stir in the powdered gelatin, lower the heat, and simmer, stirring occasionally, for an additional 8 minutes. Remove from heat and pour through a strainer to remove the herbs and shallot. Season the cream with salt and pepper.

6. Line a 1½-quart terrine or loaf pan with plastic wrap (the plastic wrap should hang at least an inch over the sides of the terrine or loaf pan) and scatter the chives on the bottom.

MAKES 6 SERVINGS

PREPARATION TIME:
20 MINUTES (PLUS 3 HOURS REFRIGERATION)

COOKING TIME:
30 TO 40 MINUTES

3 carrots, peeled and cut into thin, 4-inch sticks

2 zucchini, cut into thin, 4-inch sticks

2 white turnips, cut into thin, 4-inch sticks

1 pound green beans, tips removed

5 ounces frozen green peas

1 tablespoon unsalted butter

1 shallot, minced

¾ cup chopped fresh herbs (chives, parsley, basil, tarragon)

1 tablespoon sherry or dry white wine

2 cups heavy cream

4 packets powdered unflavored gelatin

1 tablespoon chopped chives

1 bunch radishes, thinly sliced

Salt and freshly ground black pepper

Vinaigrette (page 42)

continued

7. Cover the chives with ½ the green beans to create an even layer on the bottom of the pan. The beans should run parallel to the length of the terrine in 2 to 3 rows.

8. Lay the carrot, zucchini, and turnip sticks in a similar manner to form a compact, second layer.

9. Top with a thin layer of radishes, a layer of green peas, and a final layer of string beans.

10. Pour the warm cream over the vegetables to fill the mold. Refrigerate for at least 3 hours.

11. Turn the terrine over a serving dish and unmold by delicately lifting up the pan while holding down the exposed plastic wrap. Peel off the plastic and serve with vinaigrette drizzled atop and around each slice.

La Coupole

102, BOULEVARD MONTPARNASSE
TEL: 01 43 20 14 20
MÉTRO: VAVIN

Parisians are of two minds concerning La Coupole. The first reveres the grand café-restaurant as the quintessential Left Bank brasserie and the best vehicle short of a time machine to get within tasting distance of Montparnasse's bohemian heyday. The second laments an international academy for sidewalk intellectuals regrettably pasteurized and formularized during a 1988 restoration by new owner Jean-Paul Bucher of the Flo restaurant group. I lean toward the former view, not having seen La Coupole in 1987 (or, for that matter, 1927) and ascribing much of its lost mystique to that of Montparnasse's. Nevertheless, members of both camps may agree with me on at least one vital point: It is close to impossible to gather with close friends in an Art Deco landmark of such high energy that it pops three hundred champagne corks in a single weekend and regret you didn't go somewhere else with someone else.

That good-time guarantee is not to be taken lightly. Whereas the common wisdom of coupling dictates quieter, more intimate settings for special get-togethers, the calculating—or merely neurotic—café romantic may be wary of so secluded a locale. Here's the rub: Companions with reason to fear the disclosures, accusations, or provocations that can wreck a whole evening, if not an entire relationship, know these tend to be broached in private places. Consequently, an invitation to meet at a café where the two of you can be alone may precipitate the day when the two of you can be no longer. But a wide-open rendezvous under the bright lights of La Coupole is comparatively carefree. With your backs to the chestnut-colored (a.k.a. "La Coupole brown") velour banquettes, your giddy feet tapping the geometrically syncopated mosaic, your mouths slurping oysters, and only the famous green columns painted by thirty-two different artists to impede your desire to see and be seen together, you're inclined to feel nothing but the rapture of being in love and in Paris at the same moment.

The café romantic thus adds to his prerequisite mastery of champagnes, flowers, and perfumes a thorough knowledge of the brasserie's geography. The most desirable tables are generally those around La Coupole's *coupole* (cupola), the recessed dome in the middle of the immense brasserie and directly above a circular buffet supporting a sculpture of four figures joined at the heels, foreheads, and backs of the hand. The polished waiters and the knowing habitués they serve refer to this section as *"la centrale"* and identify the preferred café option of sitting as collaborators side by side, rather than as adversaries directly opposite one another, as *"vue-sur-la-mer"*—seaside view. A pair of Americans requesting from *directeur* Jean-Christophe Trubert a *vue-sur-la-mer* table near *la centrale*, perhaps number 99 or number 106, just might startle a young host as debonair as any Noel Coward invention whose job it is to be surprised by nothing and prepared for everything. That isn't to suggest he'd go so far as to sacrifice to nonregulars either of those enviable tables. But Trubert might recommend to visitors of such uncommon erudition the discreet corner tables 167 and 168, frequently put aside for shy notables, or table 103, where the whole world is in front of you and there's never a need to check your back.

The menu, despite many decent brasserie standards (choucroute, steak tartare, cassoulet, lamb curry, grilled steaks), superb *soupe de poisson* (saffron-scented Provençal fish soup), and classic *sole meunière*, offers nothing approaching the excitement of its raw bar selections and magnificent multitiered shellfish platters. Two or three good friends, assuming they're not overly competitive, can share without incident the 298-franc (about $50) "Plateau Prestige." It features a langoustine (a half lobster), half a crab, twelve Brittany oysters, four clams, four *bulots* (wondrous snails three to five inches long), four dog-cockles, four Spanish mussels, and handfuls of *big-orneaux* (one-inch cooked snails) and the tiny shrimp called *crevettes grises*. La Coupole employs seven men of North African origin, as almost everyone in the trade now is, in its shellfish department to assemble these *plateaux fruits de mer:* five uniformed *écaillers* (shuckers), one *sous-chef écailler,* and one *chef écailler.* Serious business.

The elimination of both the outdoor terrace and the paper-covered tables near the bar where the likes of Picasso, Hemingway, Man Ray, James Joyce, Gertrude Stein, and Jean Cocteau once converged has reduced La Coupole's function as a traditional café. The diligence required of a creative genius devoting weeks to painting a single square inch of canvas, days to penning a single sentence, or hours to nursing a single glass of lemon soda on a café-terrace is, to put it delicately, underappreciated by a corporate management with a greater interest in turning tables. The famous Le Bar Américain now operates mostly as a *bar d'attente* (waiting bar) where diners may stand for a short while and order aperitifs before being seated. Longer stays, other than during breakfast and off-hours, are discouraged.

Happily, tables on the glass-enclosed terrace are reserved at all hours for beverage-only, unclocked service. A morning coffee at the counter of the café that in 1927 became, after Le Dôme and La Rotunde, the boulevard's third great literary hemisphere, today costs 5 francs (about 80 cents)—the least expensive on Montparnasse and one of the best-kept secrets in Paris.

LA COUPOLE: Provençal Fish Soup with Spicy Garlic Sauce and Croutons *(page 33)*, Rouille *(page 34)*, Sole Meunière *(page 88)*

PROVENÇAL FISH SOUP WITH SPICY GARLIC SAUCE AND CROUTONS

SOUPE DU PÊCHEUR DE POISSON SA ROUILLE ET SES CROUTONS

One of the great rituals in participatory café-brasserie dining, La Coupole's Provençal fish soup presents you with the standard accessories kit of croutons (toasted baguette slices), grated Gruyère cheese, and *rouille* (spicy garlic mayo) as its aromatic vapors transport you away to old Marseille. Diners, once they've overcome their initial dizziness from the powerful scent of saffron, garlic, fennel, fresh herbs, seafood, and pastis (a licorice-flavored aperitif), are expected to top some croutons with a little grated Gruyère and a dab of *rouille*, float them in the soup, and go to work. Speaking of work, the use in this recipe of fish bones and fish heads makes for plenty of it during the pureeing and straining phases. Using only fish fillets will eliminate some of the effort, but also, unfortunately, some of the flavor.

1. Heat the olive oil in a big stockpot over medium heat, add the onions, carrot, fennel, celery, garlic, and bouquet garni, and combine thoroughly with the olive oil. Cover the pot, lower the heat, and cook for 20 minutes.

2. Cut the fish into large pieces. Add the fish, trimmings, and fish heads to the soup pot, raise the heat, and cook uncovered, stirring occasionally, for 5 minutes.

3. Add the tomato paste and cook an additional 5 minutes.

4. Pour in the white wine to deglaze the pot and cook until the liquid is reduced by half, 20 to 25 minutes.

5. Add the water and salt and bring to a boil. Lower the heat, and cook at a simmer, adjusting the heat as necessary, for 30 minutes. Remove the bouquet garni, fish heads, and larger bones.

MAKES 8 SERVINGS

PREPARATION TIME: 20 MINUTES (PLUS 10 MINUTES TO PREPARE THE ROUILLE)

COOKING TIME: 1 HOUR 30 MINUTES

3 tablespoons olive oil

2 medium onions, chopped

1 medium carrot, chopped

1 fennel bulb, trimmed and chopped

1 stalk celery, thinly sliced

1 clove garlic

1 bouquet garni (thyme, parsley, bay leaf)

1½ pounds fresh fish (such as haddock, halibut, monkfish, swordfish, flounder, whiting, sea bass, red snapper, or sole), whole fish filleted, heads and trimmings rinsed under cold water and reserved

3 to 4 additional fish heads (of the above fish)

2 tablespoons tomato paste

2 cups dry white wine (such as Mâcon)

2 quarts water

Salt

Cayenne pepper

continued

33

6. Transfer the rest to a food processor or blender, working with ½ or even ⅓ of the soup mixture at a time. Puree until the soup has a mostly smooth, pastelike consistency.

7. Pass through a sieve (not too fine) with firm pressure from a pestle to crush the remaining fish bones and extract all their juices.

8. Reheat the soup if necessary, season with salt, cayenne pepper, and, if desired, pastis. Ladle the soup into 8 bowls and serve. Pass the croutons, Gruyère, and *rouille* in their serving dishes.

1 teaspoon pastis (such as Pernod or Ricard; optional)

1 baguette, cut into thin slices and toasted

1 cup grated Gruyère (or Swiss) cheese

Rouille (below)

ROUILLE

A traditional garnish for Provençal fish soup and also for the fish stew *bouillabaisse, rouille* is a spicy garlic mayonnaise with a base of bread crumbs or, as in the simplified recipe below, cooked potato.

1. Cook the potato in boiling water until soft, 20 to 25 minutes. Drain and let cool.

2. Place the potato in a food processor with the egg yolks, garlic, and chili pepper and puree until smooth, about 30 seconds.

3. Slowly add the olive oil drop by drop. When the olive oil is fully incorporated, add the saffron, salt, and, if desired, a little fish soup. Transfer to a serving bowl or jar, cover, and refrigerate until ready to use.

MAKES 1¼ CUPS

PREPARATION TIME: 10 MINUTES

COOKING TIME: 20 MINUTES

1 potato (Idaho russet or Yukon gold), peeled

2 egg yolks

5 cloves garlic

1 to 2 small red chili peppers, minced

1 cup olive oil

1 pinch saffron

Salt

2 tablespoons Provençal Fish Soup (page 33; optional)

LE BISTROT DU PEINTRE

116, AVENUE LEDRU-ROLLIN

TEL: 01 47 00 34 49

MÉTRO: LEDRU-ROLLIN

At 3:38 P.M. on a clear, cold, winter afternoon, a setting sun shines a small patch of orange light cut to the slender dimensions of Le Bistrot du Peintre's west-facing terrace. A shivering couple huddled on caned chairs behind empty coffee cups and full ashtray, their faces gleaming like Day-Glo pumpkins, show no signs of departing any sooner than the sun. They must believe that the southeast corner of avenue Ledru-Rollin and rue de Charonne is somehow blessed and perhaps, for a few fleeting moments, the sacred site of the chosen café, God's *quartier général*.

Owner Didier Alaux, who also owns Pause Café, and his lithe, muscular-legged staff would surely disagree. Their lives are cursed by the number 19, as in the sum of steps on the steep spiral staircase leading to the café's upstairs dining room and shoebox kitchen. Le Bistrot du Peintre may be among Paris's most beautiful Art Nouveau cafés, but it is also one of its most narrow. On rainy days, you need to close your umbrella before stepping inside.

But what's hell for waiters is heaven for the waited-upon. The café's glass-and-iron awning overhangs a triangular slab of Paris circa 1902: sinuous woodwork framing Art Nouveau windows, mirrors, tiles, and moldings; a long, gently curving bar with brass inlays and wood-and-glass cabinetry etched with the words *"café,"* *"chocolat chaud,"* *"casse-croûte au pain de cam-*

pagne" (snacks on country bread), and *"specialiste de vin de Saumur,"* a distinction indicated by the bistro's former name, Au Vrai Saumur (At the True Saumur). The café was also known as Carrefour Bouchez and La Palette de Bastille, which is important to know if you are meeting an old friend—or picking up the apartment key he has left for you—at a so-called café. Parisians don't always recognize the name changes of a favorite local rendezvous. Looking over the list of cafés to be featured in this book, a good friend was shocked to discover I had included Le Bistrot du Peintre but not La Palette de Bastille.

Inspired perhaps by the café's architect, chef Frédérique Renoux makes the menu seem a lot bigger than it is. The selection of *tartines* (one-sided toasted sandwiches), steaks, and other bistro standards is supplemented by a couple of daily specials showing regional and seasonal standards in a new afternoon light: *joues de veau* (veal cheeks) braised with olives and carrots, dill-spiced salmon tartare, *crépinette de volaille* (flat poultry sausage) with garlic and thyme, *brandade* (salt cod puree) paired with fresh cod.

Yet the owner does not appreciate those resourceful lunches and dinners as much as Monday mornings, when he alone is behind the bar, serving coffees and croissants to the artists, craftsman, office workers, and businesspeople who are his regulars. Aside from not having to make repeated round-trips on the spiral staircase, he likes the camaraderie.

"I shake the hand of 85 percent of my clients," he says, meaning he knows them and not to suggest he spurns the other 15 percent. "That makes me happy."

WATERCRESS SOUP WITH POACHED EGGS

VELOUTÉ DE CRESSON À L'OEUF POCHÉ

This velvety watercress soup is terrific even minus the drama of the poached egg.

1. To prepare the soup, cook the onion, celery, and leek in a saucepan in 1 tablespoon of the butter over medium heat until softened but not browned.

2. Add the 2 quarts water and sea salt and bring to a boil. Add the potatoes and watercress. Simmer 1 hour.

3. Pour the soup into a food processor and blend until the mixture is an even green color and all of the elements are pureed, about 2 to 3 minutes. Return the soup to the pan, add the crème fraîche (or sour cream), and season to taste with salt and pepper. Keep warm.

4. To prepare the eggs, bring the 3 cups water to a boil in a shallow pan. Add the vinegar.

5. Break the eggs into the water, poach for 3 minutes, remove with a slotted spoon, and delicately place in serving bowls, 1 to each bowl.

6. Ladle the soup over the eggs and serve immediately.

MAKES 6 SERVINGS

PREPARATION TIME:
20 MINUTES

COOKING TIME:
1 HOUR 15 MINUTES

FOR THE SOUP

1 white onion, chopped

1 stalk celery, chopped

1 leek, white part only, cleaned and chopped

2 tablespoons unsalted butter

2 quarts water

2 teaspoons coarse sea salt or kosher salt

3 medium-sized potatoes, peeled and chopped

1 bunch watercress, washed and stems removed (3 cups leaves)

2 tablespoons crème fraîche (page 17) or sour cream

Salt and freshly ground black pepper

FOR THE POACHED EGGS

3 cups water

3 tablespoons white wine vinegar

6 eggs

Sides

CAULIFLOWER AU GRATIN

GRATIN DE CHOU-FLEUR

Chef Bruno Neveu's neat trick of wrapping the cauliflower florets and flattening them gives the gratin a firm and compact texture rather than the usual bumpy one. A recipe for classic béchamel sauce is hidden in the directions for Mornay sauce; simply eliminate the egg yolk and grated cheese.

1. In a large kettle, bring the water and salt to a rapid boil. Add the cauliflower and boil for about 10 minutes (the cauliflower should stay a little crunchy). Drain in a colander and then soak the cauliflower in cold water to stop the cooking and thus retain its texture.

2. When cool, wrap the cauliflower in a towel and press down to flatten the florets into compact tiles.

3. To prepare the Mornay sauce, melt the butter in a saucepan over low heat. Add the flour and whisk briskly for 2 minutes.

4. Add the milk, continuing to whisk briskly. When the sauce comes to a boil, season with salt, pepper, and nutmeg.

5. Add the Gruyère to this béchamel sauce, remove from heat, and mix in the egg yolk.

6. Preheat the oven to 375°F.

7. Put the cauliflower in a buttered casserole or gratin dish (about 8 inches), cover with the Mornay sauce, and sprinkle with the reserved grated cheese.

8. Bake in the oven until lightly browned, about 20 minutes.

MAKES 4 SERVINGS

PREPARATION TIME:
15 MINUTES

COOKING TIME: 45 MINUTES

6 quarts water

2 tablespoons salt

1 bunch cauliflower, leaves removed, washed, and cut into florets

FOR THE MORNAY SAUCE
(MAKES 2 CUPS)

3 tablespoons unsalted butter, plus more for greasing the casserole

1/3 cup flour

2 cups milk

Salt and freshly ground black pepper

A pinch of ground nutmeg

1/2 cup grated Gruyère or Swiss cheese, reserving 1 tablespoon to sprinkle over gratin

1 egg yolk

WHATEVER YOU'RE DRINKING,
IT'S ALL *LIMONADE*

To the French public, a *limonade* is nothing more than a sweet lemon soda, the Gallic counterpart to 7UP and Sprite. But within the hospitality business, *limonade* is a universal term for the commerce of selling beverages. *Service limonade* refers both to the work station where drinks are assembled and, more generally, the entire liquid side of the café-hotel-restaurant (CHR) trade. If a bistro has no *service limonade* or is closed during mealtimes for *service limonade*, that indicates its tables are available only to diners. But if certain tables are reserved for *service limonade* (usually the ones without table settings or cloths), that means its occupants can order beverages without food if they so please and thus regard the premises as a café even if that word does not appear in its name or on its storefront.

The term comes from the street merchants of yore who, carting soft drinks on their backs, were known as *limonadiers*. When the Auvergnats in the business of selling water, coal, wood, and wines added cold drinks to their wares, they too became known as *limonadiers*. Café waiters, managers, and proprietors all came to share the distinction of being *limonadiers*, and what an important distinction theirs is. From daybreak espressos to eleventh-hour nightcaps, coffee breaks to champagne toasts, aperitifs to after-dinner drinks, cold beers to hot *chocolats*, white Burgundies to Johnnie Walker Reds, *limonadiers* provide the fuels that mobilize,

maintain, and give closure to every café experience. Morning or night, meal or snack, planned rendezvous or chance encounter, absorbing conversation or thoughtful silence, nothing is possible without a cup of this or a glass of that.

But why *"limonadier"* and not *"cafetier,"* as the occupation is also known? Ironically, coffee did not become the defining beverage of Parisian cafés until around 1950, when modern espresso machines gained popularity. Before World War II, most coffees served in cafés were eye-openers spiked with rum or the great apple cider brandy from Normandy, calvados. In the hierarchy of French brandies, calvados ranks just below cognac and Armagnac and above such clear-colored *eaux-de-vie* as framboise (raspberry), poire Williams (pear), mirabelle (golden plum), and kirsch (wild cherry). Although most brandies are consumed after the meal as a *digestif*, calvados may also be taken between courses of a heavy dinner as a *trou normand*, which is said to open a *trou* (hole) for more food. Liqueurs, including herb-based Chartreuse, Izarra, and Benedictine, orange-flavored Grand Marnier and Cointreau, anisette-flavored Marie Brizard, and black-currant-flavored *crème de cassis* are also requested as after-dinner drinks.

At the opposite end of the meal are the appetite-enhancing *apéritifs*. Among the classic French *"apéros"* are those in the category of *quinquina*, which are slightly bitter, wine-based tonics infused with quinine. Some of the more common *quinquina* brands are St. Raphaël, Byrrah, and the French vermouths Dubonnet and Noilly Prat. (When you order a "martini" in France, you get a glass of Martini-brand vermouth and not the gin cocktail in which it is mixed.) Another category of *apéro* is licorice-flavored pastis, the specialty of Marseille requested under such brand names as Ricard, Pernod, Pastis 51, Berger, and Casanis and customarily diluted with water.

Alternative *apéros*—or anytime cold beverages—are prepared by adding sweet liqueurs and syrups to glasses of wine, beer, water, and *limonade*. A *kir* consists of dry white wine and a bit of *crème de cassis*. A beer mixed with grenadine (pomegranate-flavored syrup) is called a *tango;* add *limonade* and it becomes a *monaco,* which,

minus the grenadine, is known as a *panaché*. A *diabolo* refers to a *limonade* flavored with any syrup, the two common varieties being the *diabolo menthe* (mint) and the *diabolo grenadine*. The ever-present soft drinks are Coke (ordered as "Coca"), Orangina, Schweppes (tonic water), fruit juices, mineral water, and, from whence it all started, *limonade,* which is either poured from the tap (of variable quality) or served in a small bottle from one of several French brands.

Finally, although *limonade* covers it all, the one thing it does not indicate is American lemonade. To get a noncarbonated lemon drink you must order either a *citronnade* or a *citron pressé* (freshly squeezed lemon juice) served with water and sugar.

DECADENT MASHED POTATOES

PURÉE DE POMMES DE TERRE

Chef Jacques Barbery tries to outdo the renowned Joël Robuchon by creating a ultra-rich potato puree that gets 49 percent of its volume from butter and cream. (Any higher and he'd have to rename it mashed butter and cream with potatoes.) Whereas Robuchon's famous recipe calls for a 1 to 4 butter-potato ratio, Barbery's 3 to 10 ratio is slightly higher. Robuchon, the master, adds a cup or so of whole milk; Barbery replaces it with a slightly smaller quantity of light cream. Finally, Barbery's mashed potatoes are finished off with a drizzle of extra-virgin olive oil.

1. Scrub the potatoes, place them in a large pot, cover them by at least 1 inch with cold salted water (2 teaspoons salt per quart of water), and bring to a boil. Simmer uncovered over medium heat until the potatoes are tender, 20 to 25 minutes.

2. Drain the potatoes and while still warm (but not too hot to handle), peel them and pass them through the finest grid of a food mill into a large saucepan. Cook over low heat, stirring continuously with a wooden spatula, to dry them, 4 to 5 minutes. Add the butter little by little, stirring vigorously until fully incorporated.

3. Heat the cream in a saucepan over high heat to just under a boil. Slowly add the cream to the potatoes, stirring vigorously, until fully absorbed. Season with salt.

4. Immediately before serving, stir in the olive oil and nutmeg.

MAKES 6 SERVINGS

PREPARATION TIME:
10 MINUTES

COOKING TIME: 40 MINUTES

2 pounds Idaho russet or
   Yukon Gold potatoes

Salt

1¼ cups unsalted butter, cut
   into small pieces

¾ to 1 cup light cream

2 teaspoons extra-virgin
   olive oil

1 pinch ground nutmeg

THREE-WAY VINAIGRETTE

SAUCE DE TROIS VINAIGRES

The answer to the question asked of Café de la Musique waiters: "What's that great vinaigrette you put in your salads?"

Combine all the ingredients except salt and pepper in a bowl and whisk well. Season with salt and pepper and whisk again. Use sparingly with salads, cold vegetable terrines (page 29), and stuffed artichokes (page 22). Pour in a tight-lidded jar and store in the refrigerator.

MAKES ABOUT 2 CUPS

PREPARATION TIME:
1 MINUTE

1/4 cup red wine vinegar

1/4 cup sherry vinegar

2 tablespoons balsamic vinegar

1 1/2 cups olive oil (or vegetable oil)

1 tablespoon soy sauce

Salt and freshly ground black pepper

MA BOURGOGNE

19, PLACE DES VOSGES
TEL: 01 42 78 44 64
MÉTRO: ST-PAUL

Is it a special challenge," I, the café romantic, asked Aimé Cougoureux, the Auvergnat owner of Ma Bourgogne, "to run a café in place des Vosges, the oldest square in Paris and one of the most enchanted public spaces in all of Europe?"

"Better here than in place République," he quipped, as if that gray labyrinth of crisscrossing Métros, taxis, and pedestrians were more distant than Philadelphia. Cougoureux, I soon gathered, would sooner be judged by his secluded and rarefied address than by what is accomplished within it. How bourgeois! Ma Bourgogne thus takes its personality from place des Vosges—hardly an unpleasant notion—and not from the guy behind its counter.

The picturesque café, which opened in the 1870s as the Tabac de la Place des Vosges, is a snug fit for the northwest corner of the square. Exposed stones and wooden beams bolster the elbow-to-elbow interior. The lovely ninety-seat terrace, situated in the arcades connecting the square's matching pink-brick houses, is equipped with thirteen of the *parasols chauffants*—literally: "heating parasols"—that winterize outdoor cafés throughout Paris. (Ma Bourgogne's terrace shuts down only in February.) The problem with these gas-heated stanchions is that Parisians, particular as they are, do not care to spin around in place like chickens roasting on a rotisserie. As a result, the *parasol* not only warms but very nearly cooks one side of their heads, necks, and shoulders while the rest of their bodies go numb and their toes deep-freeze.

The café, no matter the season, is most serene on weekday mornings, when locals and tourists strolling the Marais quarter stop in for coffee or *petit déjeuner*. At 11:30 A.M., the garçons begin setting the tables for lunch. Beverage-only service resumes at 3 P.M. and again after dinner. The low-key bistro menu with high-rent prices usually has a decent plat du jour or two to go with substantial stews that augment the work of the *parasols*. Fearless Americans who opt for specialty meats, rather than the habitually safe roast chicken, are sure to get special attention from amiable co-chefs Franck Buée and Hervé Mouraut. Since their tripe is particularly good, I'd say, if you're going to have it, "Better here than (. . .)."

MA BOURGOGNE: Croquettes of Pureed Potatoes and Choux Paste *(page 44)*, Boeuf Bourguignon *(page 70)*

CROQUETTES OF PUREED POTATOES AND CHOUX PASTE

POMMES DAUPHINE

These delectable deep-fried potato croquettes, lightened by the addition of puffy *choux* pastry, are an amusing accompaniment to any number of meat and chicken dishes. Leftovers can be reheated in the oven.

1. Preheat the oven to 350°F.

2. Scrub the potatoes, place them in a large pot, cover them by at least 1 inch with cold salted water (2 teaspoons salt per quart of water), and bring to a boil. Simmer uncovered over medium heat until potatoes are tender, 20 to 25 minutes. Peel while still hot, mash, and place in the preheated oven for 5 minutes to dry out.

3. Combine the potatoes and the *choux* paste, mixing thoroughly. Season with salt and pepper.

4. Heat the oil in a deep-fryer to 350°F (not higher), or alternatively you can heat 4 inches of oil in a large pot. Fry the balls until golden brown, 4 to 7 minutes. Drain on paper towels.

MAKES 6 TO 8 SERVINGS

PREPARATION TIME: 10 MINUTES (PLUS 15 MINUTES FOR MAKING THE PASTRY)

COOKING TIME: 35 MINUTES

2 pounds Idaho russet or Yukon Gold potatoes

Salt

2½ cups Choux Paste (recipe follows)

Salt and freshly ground black pepper

Vegetable oil for deep-frying

CHOUX PASTE

PÂTE À CHOUX

Pâte à choux is the light, delicately crisp cream-puff pastry that is frequently used for éclairs and other vessels for pastry cream, whipped cream, custard, or, as in Chocolate Profiteroles (page 156), ice cream. In *pommes dauphine* it serves to lighten the potato croquette mixture.

1. Put the water, butter, sugar, and salt into a saucepan and bring to a boil over high heat. Reduce the heat to medium and simmer until the butter has melted, approximately 1 minute.

2. Add the flour all at once and stir vigorously with a wooden spoon until the dough comes away from the sides of the pan and forms a ball, 20 to 30 seconds. Remove from the heat.

3. Stir in 3 of the eggs, one by one, thoroughly incorporating each egg before the next one is added. Break the remaining egg into a small bowl, beat it, and pour ½ to ¾ into the pastry, enough to make a soft and shiny mixture.

Note: *If you are making dessert choux,* reserve the remainder of the final egg to glaze the choux before baking.

MAKES 2 ½ CUPS DOUGH

PREPARATION AND
PRECOOKING TIME:
15 MINUTES

1 cup water

*6 tablespoons unsalted
    butter*

1 teaspoon sugar

½ teaspoon salt

*1 cup plus 2 tablespoons
    flour, sifted*

4 eggs

CAFÉ RAKO

34, RUE ST-DOMINIQUE
TEL: 01 45 50 23 39
MÉTRO: INVALIDES, ASSEMBLÉE NATIONALE

The secluded charm of Café Rako is more easily enjoyed than explained. Despite a prime location just one block from the Esplanades des Invalides and its magnificent vista of what the Michelin guide calls "the most outstanding single monumental group in Paris," the intimate, two-level space lay vacant for four years before Jean-Pierre Rakoff, the curious owner of a nearby sandwicherie, signed a lease in the fall of 1995. Moreover, nothing that Rakoff has brought to the café in the way of French food and wines, Italian coffee, and multinational hospitality has altered the address's apparent invisibility to the hundreds of French and foreign sightseers always nearby.

Such obscurity has its charms, especially if you're not the one paying the rent. With its menu of carefully chosen cheeses, charcuterie, and regional wine finds as well as chef Patrice Chanet's modest but honest bistro classics, Café Rako has come to resemble a small French country house secretly hidden among the departmental buildings of France's national government. And since the Ministry of Culture is close by, the bureaucrats counted among the café's regulars tend to be creative types who work in dance, theater, and music. There's a Bohemia that circu-

lates around Rako's circular cherrywood bar, only it's the state-sponsored kind.

For a homey feel with classic and contemporary influences, Rakoff and his wife, Kim, decorated the upstairs dining rooms of this seventeenth-century building with mahogany furnishings, sisal-like carpeting, and a sunny, orange-yellow patina. Punched metal sconces illuminate two paintings in which Cubist painter Michel Thompson depicts café scenes with people who are inexplicably faceless, as Café Rako remains to the outside world.

GRATIN OF STUFFED ARTICHOKE HEARTS

GRATIN DES CAPUCINS

Gratin des Capucins was cooked up by Rako's Patrice Chanet while working at an abbey in the French Alps. He named his enlightened invention, a gratin of artichoke hearts stuffed with spinach and black currants, after the Capuchins—an order of Franciscan monks—who cultivated artichokes there. It is a versatile vegetable accompaniment that suits most red meats and poultry dishes.

1. Preheat the oven to 375°F.

2. In a saucepan over medium heat, melt 3 tablespoons of the butter, add the spinach, and cook for 5 minutes.

3. Transfer the spinach to a bowl, add the black currants, heavy cream, and nutmeg, and salt and pepper to taste, and mix well.

4. Arrange the artichoke hearts in a buttered baking dish and fill each with the spinach mixture. Sprinkle with the cheese, dot with the remaining 1 tablespoon butter cut into small pieces, and bake in the oven until the cheese browns lightly, about 15 minutes. Serve immediately.

MAKES 6 SERVINGS

PREPARATION TIME:
15 MINUTES

COOKING TIME: 20 MINUTES
(PLUS 45 MINUTES
TO COOK ARTICHOKES)

4 tablespoons ($^1\!/_2$ stick)
unsalted butter, plus more
for greasing baking dish

$^1\!/_3$ pound spinach, washed
and chopped

$^1\!/_4$ cup dry black currants
(substitute raisins)

3 tablespoons heavy cream

A pinch of ground nutmeg

Salt and freshly ground
black pepper

6 large artichoke hearts
(follow directions for
cleaning and cooking
artichokes and cutting
away the hearts on
page 22)

$^1\!/_3$ cup shredded Gruyère or
cheddar cheese

CAFÉ DE LA MUSIQUE

221, AVENUE JEAN-JAURÈS
TEL: 48 03 15 91
MÉTRO: PORTE DE PANTIN

Were it a symphony orchestra and not a café/brasserie/bar/cocktail lounge/reading room, Café de la Musique would be a guest conductor's worst nightmare. Musicians from all over the planet arrive whenever they want, sit wherever they please, and position their arched-back wooden seats, cozy velour armchairs, or conical footstools in every conceivable direction. Some play loudly in small ensembles or chamber groups; others more quietly in duet or solo. And while every player receives the identical score, its various parts are never evenly distributed. During some performances, the French kitchen goes bonkers listening to continuous repetitions of the American classical standard "Club Sandwich," with only an occasional recital of "Soupe à l'Oignon" to break the rhythm.

Yet the disorder and dissonance are most welcome in a contemporary café orchestrated by two champions of modernism, restaurateur Gilbert Costes and Pritzker Prize–winning architect Christian de Portzamparc (the two also collaborated on Café Beaubourg). Their Café de la Musique has served since December 1995 as the central meeting/eating place less for a specific residential neighborhood than for a park and a "city." The latter is de Portzamparc's Cité de la Musique, the new performance arts complex situated in the city of Paris's largest park, La Villette.

The café's 250-seat outdoor terrace faces out from Cité de la Musique, providing an expansive, motor-vehicle-free view of La Villette's place de la Fontaine aux Lions. La Grande Halle, a massive cast-iron marketplace constructed in 1867 as a venue for cattle auctions, serves as the backdrop. Hundreds of small, ground-level lamps are hidden around the cobblestone plaza, surrounding the Lion Fountain at night with a Milky Way of stars.

Inside the café, those not too caught up in their conversations, newspapers, daydreams, or the great view out the window can admire how de Portzamparc and his wife, Elizabeth, also an architect, have responded to the clientele's often conflicting needs. De Portzamparc is a proponent of fragmented, asymmetrical architecture that is nonetheless easy to get comfortable with, and this is certainly reflected in the layout of the 180-seat room. The decor is partitioned by moods, not walls. Couples who come for discreet romance are drawn to the warm, wood-walled lounge area to the right of the bar. Those who come for the sights prefer the brighter tables near the windows. Those who come to be seen sit in the turquoise and burgundy chairs or apricot-colored banquettes located in between.

Café de la Musique's most difficult balancing act is performed by chef Christophe Chaumeny. I refer not to the challenge of harmonizing the standards of French *cuisine familiale* (onion soup, leeks vinaigrette, red meat) with the lighter, international fare (spinach salad, club sandwiches, Tunisian *bricks*, quesadillas) now popular in similarly stylish and pricey cafés. What should keep this chef awake at night are

the weather reports. If Météo France predicts a cool, rainy Sunday, Chaumeny can plan on 100 to 150 customers—practically a vacation day. But if the forecast is wrong and Parc de la Villette's grounds are bathed in sunshine, he may instead serve over 1,000 covers. Imagine doing the food prep work for a Sunday picnic in the park, not knowing if you were feeding 100 or 1,000.

CAFÉ DE LA MUSIQUE: Three-Way Vinaigrette *(page 42)*, French Fries *(page 50)*

FRENCH FRIES

POMMES FRITES

MAKES 4 TO 6 SERVINGS

PREPARATION TIME:
10 MINUTES

COOKING TIME: 30 MINUTES

*2 pounds Idaho russet or
  Yukon Gold potatoes,
  peeled*

Vegetable oil for deep-frying

Salt

Each of Gilbert Costes' three cafés features a different house potato: *purée de pommes de terre* (mashed potatoes) at Le Café Marly (page 18), *pommes Dauphin* (potato pancakes) at Café Beaubourg, and golden *pommes frites* (French fries) at Café de la Musique.

1. Cut the potatoes into fries just over ⅓ inch in thickness using a french fry knife or the french fry blade of a food processor. Wash the fries well in cold water, drain, and pat very dry with a paper towel.

2. Pour enough oil into a deep-fryer or heavy skillet to reach a little over halfway up the sides of the pan, and heat to 310°F. Plunge ⅓ of the potatoes into the hot oil and cook until they stiffen and start to color, 6 to 8 minutes. Lift up the fries and set aside on paper towels for up to several hours at room temperature. Repeat with the second and then final batches of fries.

3. A few minutes before serving, increase the oil temperature to 360°F. Drop in all the fries at once and cook until crisp and golden brown, 2 to 3 minutes. Lift out, drain on paper towels, sprinkle with salt, and serve.

With little time and manpower during busy service hours for elaborate preparation and fussy presentation, many of the finest café-bistros and brasseries rely more on their prowess in gathering the best meats and seafood than for preparing them. This, a defining emphasis of their rough-and-ready cuisine, is especially true of the *grillades*—grilled meats, principally beef—which require minimal effort in the kitchen but are nevertheless adored by the many Parisian diners who do not fear red meat as a cardiovascular time bomb, especially in 5- to 6-ounce portions. The greatness and sophistication of French gastronomy does not rule out the pleasures of a juicy, no-nonsense steak optimally paired with real fries; it embraces them.

I have not included any recipes for *grillades*, since these would entail mostly listing the addresses of some good butchers. But it's perhaps helpful to outline the most adored French cuts of beef for the purposes of grilling, pan-broiling, and pan-frying: *faux-filet, onglet, entrecôte, bavette, romsteck,* and *côte de boeuf.*

Faux-filet—A prized cut from the short loin, *faux-filet* is extremely juicy and toothsome and nearly as tender as filet mignon. Its American counterpart is known both as shell steak and New York strip steak.

Onglet—A small, select cut from just below the loin, tender and flavorful *onglet* (hanger steak) typically appears on menus followed by the words *"à l'échalotte"*—indicating it is covered with a sauce of minced shallots.

Entrecôte—The equivalent of extremely tender rib-eye, *entrecôte* rarely makes an appearance in a bistro without some sort of sauce accompaniment, usually a *bordelaise* consisting of red wine, shallots, butter, and fresh herbs.

Bavette—Juicy, lean, tough, and fibrous, *bavette* is the portion of the flank closest to short loin. It should not be confused with *flanchet*, which is also part of the flank, and is used primarily in stews.

Romsteck (also *rumsteak*)—From the top butt or rump portion, *romsteck* (rump steak) is tender and tasty and may be cut into thick slices for grilling and pan-frying.

Côte de boeuf—A prime piece of loin meat cut directly off the bone to a thickness of perhaps 2½ inches, *côte de boeuf* is often served for two. It's the closest thing in the vicinity of the Seine to a T-bone.

51

CAFÉ DE L'INDUSTRIE

16, RUE ST-SABIN
TEL: 01 47 00 13 53
MÉTRO: BRÉGUET-SABIN, BASTILLE

At a time when modern design was all the rage and new cafés had to be cold to be cool, Gérard Le Flem's head was lost in the tropics even when his body wasn't. To make himself feel away even when at home, the world traveler stripped down and expanded a darkened corner bistro near the Bastille, moved in the mementos from his many voyages south, and fashioned a café with the dim, decadent, dated look of a sleepy, French Colonial haunt for European exiles awaiting exit visas. Shortly after its opening in 1989, Café de l'Industrie helped inspire a new and enduring craze, the retro café. Now that similarly nostalgic enterprises are commonplace, it's difficult to recall that only a scant decade ago, replacing something that's starting to look old with something that looks much older was considered backward and, if given further thought, totally outside the Frenchman's character.

The broad appeal of Le Flem's industriousness is obvious. Old fans, clocks, radios, lamps, and blinds, Deco-patterned mirrors and frosted glass, and Oriental rugs spread over dark wood floors create an arty, meditative space that fulfills the fantasy of a bohemian café. Although the Formica bar, the lone remnant from the prior café, and the worn burgundy banquettes are clogged during and after mealtimes with smoke and chatter, the rooms are particularly inviting to solitary muses who want no other company than their notebooks and imaginations. This is one of the few literary cafés where people actually come to write literature—or their idea of it. Few mind the simple menu of salads, pastas, and French standards prepared with tropical accents (Creole codfish, tuna tartare *à la tahitienne*), particularly if they're only having an espresso. The food is inexpensive and mostly endurable and there's even the red onion confit, a jamlike steak condiment, and a prune flan to recommend.

Nevertheless, the café's popularity with women is somewhat bewildering considering how openly the owner displays his particular tastes toward the opposite sex. The honey-mustard walls exhibit a gallery of paintings, photos, and other likenesses of black nudes. Le Flem himself signed the canvas of two Haitian women. Furthermore, the sociable young waitresses are hired for their exotic appearance ("not sexy but pretty," he stipulates, though who's to say they are not both?) and inexperience. He regards trained servers as too professional, too mannered, and thus too unnatural. As such, he is extremely proud to have employed foreign waitresses, including Myrtle, an *Américaine,* who speaks no French. Not a word. Perhaps due to the high levels of unemployment in France, this unique hiring practice has yet to inspire a trend in a city that is still, despite one café's tropical palms and calm, the French capital.

RED ONION CONFIT

CONFIT D'OIGNON

Although Café de l'Industrie serves its terrific Red Onion Confit in place of fried shallots as a garnish for pan-fried *onglet* (flank steak), the sweet, jelly-like condiment may be prepared in advance, stored in the refrigerator up to several months, and used when needed as a convenient and jazzy accompaniment for a variety of meats, poultry, and fish, or simply as a spread for sandwiches, breads, and hors d'oeuvres. Try adding a dash of cayenne pepper to make it a little spicy.

1. Heat the vegetable oil in a saucepan over medium-high heat, add the onions, and cook, stirring occasionally, until golden, 4 to 5 minutes.

2. Add the red wine vinegar and the grenadine and heat to a boil.

3. Stir in the sugar and continue to boil for an additional 10 minutes. Season with salt and pepper.

4. Pour the mixture into a hot, sterilized jar and seal. Refrigerate for at least 4 hours before serving.

MAKES 1 CUP

PREPARATION TIME:
5 MINUTES (PLUS 4 HOURS REFRIGERATION)

COOKING TIME: 20 MINUTES

2 tablespoons vegetable oil

3 red onions, chopped

¼ cup red wine vinegar

¼ cup grenadine syrup

1 cup sugar

Salt and freshly ground black pepper

CRISP ZUCCHINI STICKS WITH FENNEL

BATONNETS DE COURGETTE AU FENOUIL

Aperfect match for Thomas Dufour's Sautéed Tuna Steak with Orange and Star Anise Butter Sauce (page 64). The zucchini sticks constitute a crisp delivery system for the perfume of the fennel, which in turn draws out the star anise flavor in the tuna's creamy butter sauce. The dish can also be served with a variety of Provençal and Mediterranean main courses, in which the fennel's licorice-like essence is most welcome.

1. Cut the fennel bulbs in half and remove the cores. Slice thinly.

2. In a saucepan, combine the fennel, 2 tablespoons of the olive oil, and the water, salt, and pepper. Cook over high heat for 1 minute, then reduce to low heat, cover, and cook for 20 to 25 minutes. Stir occasionally and add a little more water if it dries out completely before the cooking is complete. The fennel should be cooked thoroughly. Verify the seasoning and set aside.

3. Cut each zucchini crosswise into 3 even-length pieces. Set each cylinder upright and cut 3 even slices lengthwise. Cut these slices into three to four even sticks.

4. Heat a skillet over high heat. Add the remaining olive oil. When the olive oil is very hot, add the zucchini sticks. Season with salt and pepper and cook, stirring regularly, for about 5 minutes. The zucchini should be crisp.

5. Drain the zucchini in a colander and combine with the fennel. Serve warm immediately.

MAKES 6 SERVINGS

PREPARATION TIME:
20 MINUTES

COOKING TIME: 25 MINUTES

3 bulbs fennel, trimmed and washed

¼ cup olive oil

⅔ cup water

Salt and freshly ground black pepper

6 small, firm zucchini, washed and ends removed

BRASSERIE DES DEUX PALAIS

3, BOULEVARD DU PALAIS

TEL: 01 43 54 20 89

MÉTRO: CITÉ

Every Parisian may have his day in court and, while in recess, Brasserie des Deux Palais. Situated on the Île de la Cité directly opposite the Palais de Justice, the café counts among its regulars some of France's most distinguished judges, lawyers, politicians, and career criminals. Among the more transitory clients are debtors who, after settling their obligations at the Tribunal de Commerce, drift past the café's beautiful terrace on the rue de Lutèce like the fallen heroes in a Victor Hugo novel, ostensibly to spend their last few centimes on a loaf of bread. Yet oddly, the taste in clothes and wine exhibited by these ruined men is no less noble than that of their prosecutors.

"They are generally not in serious difficulty," says proprietor Christian Couderc, a veteran restaurateur who knows bankruptcy is hardly the same thing as poverty.

As for the lawyers, the stoics who have just lost a big case are indistinguishable from their victorious adversaries. If someone is sulking, notes Couderc, it's surely not the lawyer; it's the client.

The café is valued for its good manners, fast service, and honest but unexceptional brasserie fare: *sole meunière, andouillette* (pig intestines sausage), duck confit, choucroute, omelets, and composed salads. I admire most the vegetable purees that accompany the meats and fish, but others care only about discretion. They choose to study the details of a case—or the eyes of a romantic companion—in the narrow confines of the secluded rear dining room. Its decor, like the courtrooms across the boulevard, possesses the elegance and dignity of a prior age. The magnificent molded ceiling, ornate glasswork, and geometric mosaic date back to extensive renovations in 1927. The building served as a chapel, providing another sort of sanctuary for the same clientele, before it was converted to a tavern around the turn of the century.

Due to its central and therefore neutral location between two riverbanks and four arrondissements (First, Fourth, Fifth, and Sixth), the café is a diplomatic rendezvous for estranged partners in love, business, or crime who want to resolve their differences out of—but not very far from—court. Since it's neither Left Bank nor Right Bank, warring parties from opposite sides of the Seine can meet informally for coffee and self-arbitration without crossing into enemy territory.

BRASSERIE DES DEUX PALAIS: Red Cabbage Puree *(page 56)*, Split Pea Puree *(page 57)*

SIDES

RED CABBAGE PUREE

PURÉE DE CHOU ROUGE

What fun! The soft though not too creamy texture of a puree. The beautiful color of fresh lavender. The homey smells of cabbage and bacon. What more could you want with your main course of ham, pork, or sausage?

1. Heat 1 tablespoon of the butter in a skillet over medium-high heat, add the onions, and cook, stirring occasionally, until they begin to brown, about 10 minutes. Remove from the heat and set aside.

2. Cook the bacon in a large saucepan over medium heat for 1 minute. Add the cabbage and cook, tossing with the bacon to set in the color, about 2 minutes.

3. Add the onions, apple, wine, chicken stock, and hot water to the cabbage, season with salt and pepper, and cook, stirring occasionally, for 35 minutes.

4. Drain the cabbage mixture and puree in a food processor, using the pulse button and scraping down the sides of the container as necessary, until the cabbage is finely minced, about 30 seconds.

5. When ready to serve, reheat if necessary, and mix in the crème fraîche and remaining butter.

MAKES 6 SERVINGS
(ABOUT 3 CUPS)

PREPARATION TIME:
10 MINUTES

COOKING TIME: 45 MINUTES

3 to 4 tablespoons unsalted butter

2 small onions, sliced

4 strips bacon

1 red cabbage (about 1 pound), washed, cored, and cut into strips

1 small apple (a tart variety), peeled, cored, and sliced

1/2 cup dry white wine (such as Mâcon)

1/2 cup chicken stock

1/2 cup hot water

Salt and freshly ground black pepper

1 to 2 tablespoons crème fraîche (page 17), or sour cream

SPLIT PEA PUREE

PURÉE SAINT-GERMAIN

Describing it as yellow split pea soup with the consistency of mashed potatoes may not be the most enticing way to sell you on a side dish that's especially good when accompanying ham, pork, and sausage dishes, but it's accurate. This puree makes a perfect pair with the brasserie's lavender-colored red cabbage puree (previous recipe).

1. Peel the onion and prick it with the cloves.

2. Heat the bacon in a large saucepan over medium heat for 1 minute, add the lettuce, and cook until wilted, about 3 minutes.

3. Add the split peas, carrot, bouquet garni, potatoes, and onion pricked with cloves, cover with the water, and cook, stirring occasionally, until thickened but not dry and stiff, about 1 hour.

4. Remove the bouquet garni and onion, and season the split pea mixture with salt and pepper. Puree in a food processor until smooth, stopping and scraping down the sides of the container if necessary, about 1 minute.

5. Immediately before serving, reheat if necessary, then mix in the butter and crème fraîche, and garnish, if desired, with croutons.

MAKES 6 TO 8 SERVINGS

PREPARATION TIME: 15 MINUTES

COOKING TIME: 1 HOUR 5 MINUTES

1 onion

6 whole cloves

6 to 8 strips bacon, diced

4 large leaves lettuce

1 pound dry yellow split peas

1 carrot, diced

1 bouquet garni (thyme, parsley, bay leaf)

1 pound potatoes (2 large potatoes), peeled and cut into ½- to 1-inch cubes

1 quart water

Salt and freshly ground black pepper

1 to 2 tablespoons unsalted butter

1 to 2 tablespoons crème fraîche (page 17), or sour cream

Croutons (optional)

Café du Marché

38, RUE CLER
TEL: 01 47 05 51 27
MÉTRO: ÉCOLE MILITAIRE

Café du Marché has working in its favor wonderful potatoes sautéed in goose fat, a perfectly executed cup—or three-ounce glass—of Lavazza espresso, and the distinctive X-backed iron chairs Olivier Gagnère designed for Le Café Marly. Still, all that Jacques Maurel and Yvette Costes, the ex of Marly's Gilbert Costes, needed to make theirs a year-round destination café were the clear-plastic windscreens and four outdoor heaters that winterize the terrace and keep it in daily contact with the sights, smells, sounds, and rhythms of rue Cler.

As enjoyable as it is to walk and shop this pedestrian market street situated midway between Les Invalides and the Eiffel Tower, the surest way to absorb its village-like charms is to stop long enough to smell the coffee. Parisians know instinctively that you have to interrupt your comings and goings to appreciate what those around you are up to. The vendors who come to Café du Marché for steak lunches as early as 9:30 A.M. can take in the market from outside their shops and gossip with colleagues. Mothers can trace the latest episodes in the lives of the children they've just picked up at school over afternoon hot chocolates. American tourists perhaps visiting one of several American cultural institutions nearby can eat fat-rimmed duck and goose-fat-lathered potatoes and marvel at the high percentage of rue Cler passersby who are as thin as postcards.

My primer for Café du Marché and rue Cler concludes with these observations: Georges, the distinguished man who runs the café's crepe stand was indeed the chef de cuisine on a Greek cruise ship. The American "Caesar" salad is prepared, inexplicably, with tandoori chicken. The "80/20" ratio refers either to the proportion of arabica and robusto beans in its coffee or the makeup of locals and tourists that frequent its terrace. The dizzying, unrelenting scent of tarragon comes not from the café's kitchen but rather from the adjacent rotisserie. Of the two florists on rue Cler, the arrangements at Cler Fleurs are said to be favored by younger women; Aux Fleurs du Champs de Mars' bouquets, by mature women. This creates interesting possibilities for the middle-aged male shopper. He can go to the former florist if he's buying flowers for his wife or mother but wants to give the impression he's buying for a young mistress. He can go to the latter if he wants to accomplish the opposite result.

SAUTÉED POTATOES

POMMES SAUTÉES

MAKES 4 SERVINGS

PREPARATION TIME:
10 MINUTES

COOKING TIME: 15 MINUTES

Café du Marché employs one cook who works exclusively on potato detail, peeling, slicing, and washing the spuds in the morning and sautéeing them all day long in goose fat, which, aside from being the best manner of frying them, is lower in saturated fat than butter. But since goose fat is not readily available in American markets, I've suggested you replace it with butter, oil, or clarified butter. The café serves its sautéed potatoes with steak, duck confit, and just about every other hot dish it serves (you're encouraged to do the same). You half expect them to use them as a garnish for fruit tarts, too.

2 pounds small round red potatoes, peeled and thinly sliced

4 to 6 tablespoons unsalted butter (or substitute oil, clarified butter, or a combination of the two)

2 tablespoons chopped fresh parsley

Salt

1. Wash the potatoes in cold water, drain, and pat very dry with paper towels.

2. Melt 4 tablespoons of the butter in a skillet over medium-high heat. When the butter is very hot but not yet coloring, add the potatoes and cook, turning them often and moving around the pan, until golden on all sides, 12 to 15 minutes, being sure to regulate the heat so that the butter does not brown and adding more butter if needed.

3. Season with salt, sprinkle with parsley, drain off the excess fat (although Café du Marché rarely does), and serve.

CAFÉ WINES

The irrepressible conceit of the café-educated wine connoisseur is acquired through the discovery and appreciation of small, affordable, unsung wines found in small, affordable, unsung places. His preference is for "vins de propriétaire," the words proudly displayed in bistros to indicate that their wines were purchased directly from the producer. The practice, while not a guarantee of good quality and value, does distinguish hosts who either care about wine or, at the very least, care about attracting clients who do.

The task of choosing and tasting wines can be overwhelming if not entirely unpleasant. I've pared down the process, as most cafés do, by focusing on some prevalent alternatives to more pricey Bordeaux and Burgundy, not to suggest that you boycott bottles from those famous wine regions, but simply to alert you to the more modest wines described below. The selection reflects the Parisian preference for reds over whites, as well as for wines from vineyards along the Loire River, which flows from central France to the Atlantic. Within the café counterculture, the refreshingly fruity Loire wines are as perennially fashionable as Albert Camus paperbacks and black turtleneck sweaters.

REDS

Bourgueil—A popular wine from the Loire's Touraine region, Bourgueil is a light, fruity, at times vegetal wine with a strong bouquet and flavor suggestive of raspberries.

Saumur-Champigny—Also from the Loire, Saumur-Champigny is a light-bodied, easy-to-drink wine with a deep ruby color. It often possesses the scent of violets, blackberries, and raspberries.

Chinon—The finest Loire reds rely on the Cabernet Franc grape to create soft, flowery, and herb-tinged wines with a bouquet of raspberries and black currants.

Sancerre—Best known for its whites, Sancerre also produces pale-colored, light-bodied reds that are becoming fashionable. The fruitiness—cherry, raspberry, black currant—typical of Loire wines is extracted not from Cabernet Franc in this case but from Pinot Noir, the distinguished grape of red Burgundy.

Gamay de Touraine—Frequently served lightly chilled as an alternative to fruity Beaujolais, the wine with which the Gamay grape is most closely associated, Gamay de Touraine presents a bouquet of cherries and black currants with undercurrents of smoky, vegetal, or mildly sweet spices.

Beaujolais—Youthful, fresh wines from southern Burgundy, prized for their fruity and flowery character. Beaujolais Nouveau is a hyped category released on the third Thursday in November, just weeks after its grapes are harvested. Of lesser fame but much higher quality are the ten

Beaujolais designated as *crus* (growths): Moulin-à-Vent, Juliénas, Morgon, Chénas, Fleurie, Saint-Amour, Côte-de-Brouilly, Brouilly, Chiroubles, and Régnié.

Côtes du Rhône—This low-priced and abundantly produced wine from the Rhône Valley varies dramatically in fullness and quality. Better Côtes du Rhônes tend to have a full body, an intense, berryish bouquet, and a round, effortlessly satisfying character.

WHITES

Muscadet—An extremely crisp, dry, and affordable white esteemed as the perfect match for shellfish and seafood and as an aperitif. The best Muscadets are from the Sèvre-et-Maine region and should be drunk when young.

Sauvignon de Touraine—Less expensive than the two superior Loire whites listed below, Sauvignon (for the Sauvignon Blanc grape) de Touraine is a crisp, lively wine displaying vegetal, floral, and fruity notes.

Pouilly-Fumé—An exciting and refreshing wine with rising prices to prove it, Pouilly-Fumé has a light, crisp, tart character richly scented with grassy or earthy nuances.

Sancerre—More acidic than Pouilly-Fumé but not as full, refreshing Sancerre is adored for its crisp, zesty tang.

Mâcon—Made exclusively from Chardonnay grapes, Mâcon whites are at the low end of Burgundy, both in geography and pricing. These popular wines tend to be light, crisp, fruity, and extremely dry.

61

Main Dishes

AUX PETITS JOUEURS

8, RUE DE LA MAIN-D'OR
TEL: 01 48 05 77 10
MÉTRO: LEDRU-ROLLIN

A young couple steps up to the small bar at Aux Petits Joueurs and orders two beers, the man and woman each handing the bartender 50-franc bills. He examines the two fifties front and back, shrugs, keeps one bill—the woman's—and hands the other back to the man.

"It's the twentieth century," he explains, and the pillars of this little community—the men who never leave the bar lest it fall down—nod their approval. They obviously like the idea, however radical it is to them, of a woman buying for a man. Which end of the century he's referring to might incite greater disagreement on rue de la Main-d'Or, a block-long throwback that embraces not one but four old-fashioned bistros as contemporaries: À l'Ami Pierre, itself a treasure, at number 5, L'Oreille Cassée at number 6, Le Chaudron des Sauciers at number 10, and Aux Petits Joueurs at number 8.

The last, for decades a *bouchon,* or Lyonnais-style bistro, sold heating coal as late as 1995, when it was bought by Gil Moisson and Olivier David, two businessmen experiencing midlife crisis at the respective ages of twenty-eight and thirty. Removing the coal and its storage space lengthened the ragtag room by six feet and increased its capacity from sixteen to twenty-eight diners, now mostly in their twenties and early thirties. The new owners also mounted a red "Tabac" sign next to the kitchen door and perched a bald-headed dummy on a swing over the repositioned

bar, but left the rest unchanged, save, of course, for the vintages of the nine Beaujolais growths (*crus*) that fill the cinder-block wine rack.

Gil, the Laurel of this comic duo, directs traffic in the front of the house while Olivier, the Hardy figure, supposedly mans the kitchen. But the jovial chef is continually abandoning his post to drop in on diners, ostensibly to see how their meals are progressing but more often to join in their revelry. He sees it as his duty to greet every woman who enters as he would a friend arriving at his house, and so he kisses them all four times, twice on each cheek. Meanwhile, Gil keeps up on all the *ragot,* or gossip, on the block (most of it untrue) and is thus esteemed by daytime habitués ranging from Jackie, a pink-faced pensioner wounded during the Algerian war, to Greg, a Mohawk-haired American painter/special-effects artist who takes all his business calls on the bistro's pay phone.

With no printed menu, the nightly selection is limited to two rustic, low-priced plats du jour that are coupled to give diners what Olivier considers a real choice. His idea of a real choice is a pairing of one dish that's *difficile* and another that's *simple.* By *difficile* he means heavy hitters, often consisting of variety meats, that are not to everyone's taste—tripe, *tête de veau* (calf's head), *andouillette* (sausage made from pig's intestines). His notion of *simple* consists of more accessible classics like *blanquette de veau* (veal stew), *pot-au-feu* (boiled beef with vegetables), and *tourte auvergnate* (filled with potato, bacon, and cheese). If only decisions about work, love, and life at this end of the twentieth century could be reduced to *difficile* and *simple.*

VEAL BLANQUETTE

BLANQUETTE DE VEAU

With its creamy white sauce thickened with butter and flour, this classic French stew appears the quintessence of nutritionally incorrect food. Nevertheless, I encourage you to reduce the sauce until it's good and thick. It's better to reduce too much than not enough. Too thin is boring, at least when it comes to blanquettes. Do not be dismayed by the dish's resemblance to cafeteria glop. This is great comfort food. Trust me, you're going to love it.

1. In a bowl or baking dish, cover the veal pieces with cold water, cover, and refrigerate for 30 minutes. Drain.

2. Meanwhile, in a large pot combine the vegetables, bouquet garni, and salted water and bring to a boil over high heat. Reduce the heat to medium-low and simmer for 1 hour. Strain the vegetable broth, setting the vegetables aside.

3. In a heavy-bottomed pot over medium heat, melt the butter. Add the flour and mix with a wooden spoon for 1 minute.

4. Reduce the heat to low. Add the veal pieces and seal in the juices by cooking 1 to 2 minutes on all sides without allowing them to brown.

5. Add 5 cups of the vegetable broth and mix well. Add the white wine and bring to a boil over high heat, then reduce the heat to medium-low, cover, and simmer for 1 hour.

6. Add the cream and cook over medium heat to reduce the sauce until it's thick enough to coat the spoon, 15 to 20 minutes.

7. Add the vegetables and heat through. Season with lemon juice, nutmeg, and salt and pepper to taste. Serve with rice or boiled potatoes.

MAKES 6 SERVINGS

PREPARATION TIME:
30 MINUTES

COOKING TIME:
2 HOURS 20 MINUTES

2 pounds veal shoulder or breast, cut into 2-inch pieces

6 carrots, peeled and sliced

6 small turnips, peeled and sliced

2 large onions, sliced

2 leeks, white parts only, washed and sliced

1 bouquet garni (thyme, parsley, bay leaf)

2 quarts water combined with 1 tablespoon sea salt

3 tablespoons unsalted butter

1/4 cup flour

1 cup dry white wine (such as Mâcon)

2 cups heavy cream

Fresh lemon juice, to taste

A pinch of ground nutmeg

Salt and freshly ground black pepper

SAUTÉED TUNA STEAK WITH ORANGE AND STAR ANISE BUTTER SAUCE

Thon Beurre d'Orange et Badiane

A superb Provençal-style dish that takes only five ingredients, five cooking steps, and 30 minutes to make. Its side dish at L'Ébauchoir, Crisp Zucchini Sticks with Fennel (page 54), is, by comparison, a 45-minute ordeal.

1. Heat the orange juice, grated orange peel, and star anise in a saucepan over medium-high heat and cook the mixture to reduce it until it has the thick consistency of a syrup, about 12 to 15 minutes.

2. Add the butter and mix with a whisk.

3. Remove from the heat, extract the star anise, mix the sauce again with a whisk, season with salt and pepper, and then set aside.

4. Heat a skillet over high heat, pour in the olive oil, and then add the tuna to the pan. Sear the tuna for 2 to 4 minutes on each side, depending on the thickness.

5. Cover the tuna steaks with the orange and star anise butter sauce and serve.

MAKES 6 SERVINGS

PREPARATION TIME:
10 MINUTES

COOKING TIME: 20 MINUTES

Juice of 6 oranges

Peel of 1 orange, grated

6 star anise

*¾ cup (1½ sticks)
    unsalted butter*

*Salt and freshly ground
    black pepper*

3 tablespoons olive oil

*3 pounds tuna, cut into
    6 ½-pound steaks*

PÉTRISSANS

30 BIS, AVENUE NIEL
TEL: 01 42 27 52 03
MÉTRO: TERNES

Toward the conclusion of my first visit to Pétrissans, I was spotted at the table nearest the doorway to the adjoining boutique and its wall library of expertly chosen wines by my friend Patrick Pougeux. Content to be dining alone (who wouldn't be in the company first of buttery escargots dripping over crisp little toasts and then eggs loosely scrambled with black truffles?), I was nonetheless flattered to hear that devotee of bistro pleasures and one-upmanship call out "Daniel!" in that landmark address. But my wine-volatilized mood seesawed when he reached past my extended hand for my inexpensive bottle of Saumur-Champigny and, after inspecting its label and assessing its advanced level of depletion, ridiculed my ongoing association—at Pétrissans of all places!—with so minor a *vin rouge*.

"You have the right to a slip-up," he quipped in the argot and logic unique to Parisian bistros, "but not two in the same night." Confused by Pougeux's putdown, I perceived only that it would be difficult to show my face there again if I didn't come up with a surefooted response. I was about to deliver an eloquent spiel about the charms of simple reds in general and lightly chilled Saumur-Champigny in particular—I'd been rehearsing ones like it every morning in front of the bathroom mirror—when Marie-Christine Allemoz, the great-granddaughter of Martin Pétrissans, interceded to defend both my honor and that of the 140,000 proud inhabitants of Saumur and Champigny. Moreover, since Pougeux unwittingly belittled one of *her* selections from *her* wine list, Madame Allemoz was put in the position of upholding the reputation of a family business established in 1895. Pougeux must have understood that debating her on the subject of wine—at Pétrissans of all places!—would be committing an error a good deal more serious than any slip-up because he backed off in a hurry.

"There is pleasure to be had at all levels," Madame Allemoz later explained, stating a philosophy she and her husband, the discerning Jean-Marie Allemoz, apply both to wines and, since 1989, the dishes served in the bistro that grew out of their wine shop. Their kitchen excels at doing the basics extraordinarily well with the finest available products. Businesspeople and the well-to-do may come to rediscover such humble or hackneyed pleasures as *oeufs en gelée* (poached eggs in aspic), classic crème brûlée, and what may be the best *celeri rémoulade* (shredded celery root and spicy mayonnaise) in the French capital. Order a *faux-filet* and you get a shell steak from Salers, a *grand cru* French beef. Opt for an *andouillette* and you get a *grand cru* of pig's intestines sausage. Invest in a *grand cru* Bordeaux and you encounter a sublime wine that admittedly makes a return to a lightweight like Saumur-Champigny disheartening if not unthinkable. Pougeux did have a point.

The clublike oak furnishings (from a *grand cru* of French trees?), glass panels, and beige moldings make the bistro look much older and more elegant than it is. The bareness and informality of the dining room, four-stool bar, and terrace invite habitués to use the premises as a neighborhood rendezvous and stopover. The dandyish gourmand and art lover Alain Weill holds court nearly every night, carrying on about young chefs who, contrary to Pétrissans', impose their personalities and inventions on bistro fare and, in the process, "kill it."

"A bistro was a man in the kitchen and a woman in the dining room," Weill told me, speaking as maestro to protégé. "They didn't try to overdo it. They stuck to their roots. That's what made it a bistro."

PÉTRISSANS: Poached Eggs in Aspic *(page 4)*, Celery Root Salad with Spicy Mayonnaise *(page 7)*, Steamed Chicken with Tarragon Sauce *(page 69)*

STEAMED CHICKEN
WITH TARRAGON SAUCE

POULET À LA VAPEUR, SAUCE CRÉMÉE À L'ESTRAGON

Delicious proof of how a great French wine bistro is moving—and not moving—with the times. Although the chicken is steamed and thus appealing to lighter appetites and diets, the sauce nevertheless contains two cups of heavy cream. *Plus ça change . . .*

1. Cut the chicken into 4 pieces. Separate the thighs from the drumsticks and the wings from the breasts. Carefully remove the bones of the thighs and the breasts. Set the chicken pieces and bones aside.

2. In a large stockpot combine the carrots, leeks, onions, celery, parsley, garlic, and cloves. Add the salted water, and bring to a boil. Add the chicken bones and white wine. Bring to a boil, then reduce the heat to medium-low, and simmer for 1½ hours. Strain the broth into a saucepan.

3. Cook 1 quart of the broth over high heat to reduce by half, about 20 minutes. Add the heavy cream and reduce by half, approximately 15 minutes. Season with salt and pepper to taste.

4. Prepare a steamer large enough to cook the chicken pieces. Rub the chicken pieces with ½ of the chopped tarragon. Place in the top of the steamer and steam 15 to 20 minutes.

5. Just before serving, add the remaining tarragon to the sauce. Place the steamed chicken pieces on a platter and cover with the sauce. Serve with basmati rice.

MAKES 6 SERVINGS

PREPARATION TIME:
20 MINUTES

COOKING TIME:
2 HOURS 15 MINUTES

*One 2½- to 3-pound
   chicken*

2 carrots, peeled and diced

*2 leeks, white parts only,
   washed and diced*

2 onions, diced

1 stalk celery, diced

1 cup chopped fresh parsley

*2 cloves garlic, roughly
   chopped*

3 whole cloves

1½ quarts salted water

*1 cup dry white wine
   (such as Mâcon)*

2 cups heavy cream

*Salt and freshly ground
   pepper to taste*

*1 cup finely chopped fresh
   tarragon leaves*

MA BOURGOGNE'S

BOEUF BOURGUIGNON

I think it's all right to be from Auvergne, as proprietor Aimé Cougoureux is, and still call your place Ma Bourgogne—"My Burgundy"—providing you serve a solid version of the region's classic beef stew cooked in red Burgundy with bacon, onions, and mushrooms. You can also get away with using a good, full-bodied red wine other than pricey Burgundy, as most economically minded cafés are wont to do, without being arrested. The control laws of the *Appellation d'Origine Contrôlée* (A.O.C.) that guarantee the place of origin and superior quality of fine French wines like Burgundy do not apply, though purists might insist they should, to the dishes traditionally cooked with them. Note that the beef must be marinated a day ahead.

1. *The day before,* combine the beef, peppercorns, onions, carrots, leek, and celery in a large bowl. Pour in red wine to cover. Cover the bowl with plastic wrap and refrigerate for 24 hours.

2. Remove the meat from the marinade, reserving the marinade, and pat dry with paper towels.

3. In a heavy-bottomed pan, heat 1 tablespoon of the oil over high heat until very hot. Add ½ the meat and cook until lightly browned on all sides, approximately 4 minutes. Remove, add another tablespoon oil and repeat the browning process with the rest of the meat.

4. Return all the meat to the pan, add the tomato paste, and sprinkle with flour. Stir well over medium heat for 3 minutes.

5. Add the marinade with the vegetables, the beef stock, the bouquet garni, and the clove. Bring to a boil, reduce the heat to low, cover, and simmer for 2½ hours.

MAKES 6 SERVINGS

PREPARATION TIME (AFTER 24 HOURS MARINATION): 40 MINUTES

COOKING TIME: 3 HOURS

3 pounds stew beef (such as bottom round, pot roast, or rump roast), cut into 2-inch cubes

3 to 4 black peppercorns

3 onions, cut into large pieces

2 carrots, peeled and cut into large dice

1 leek, white part only, washed and cut into large pieces

2 stalks celery, cut into large pieces

1 bottle red Burgundy or red Côtes du Rhône

3 tablespoons vegetable oil

2 tablespoons tomato paste

¼ cup flour

1 cup beef stock or bouillon

1 bouquet garni (thyme, bay leaf, parsley)

1 clove

Salt and freshly ground black pepper

6. Remove the cover and cook until the meat is tender, about ½ hour more. During this time, regularly skim off the grease that has risen to the surface.

7. Remove the meat from the sauce. Strain the sauce through a fine sieve and boil over high heat for 10 minutes. Season with salt and pepper. Return the meat to the sauce.

8. In a small saucepan, cover the bacon with cold water. Bring to a boil and drain immediately. Heat the remaining 1 tablespoon oil in a skillet. Add the bacon and fry over high heat for 3 minutes. Add to the beef.

9. In the same skillet, add the sliced mushrooms and cook over high heat for 5 minutes, stirring regularly. Add to the beef.

10. Stir well, and serve with boiled potatoes.

5 strips thick-cut bacon, cut into 1- to 1½-inch sticks (lardons)

4 cups sliced fresh mushrooms

AU GÉNÉRAL LA FAYETTE'S

CROQUE MONSIEUR

MAKES 4 SERVINGS

PREPARATION TIME:
5 MINUTES

COOKING TIME: 15 MINUTES

At most Paris cafés, the *croque monsieur*—the French ham-and-cheese—is no longer prepared as a square sandwich but rather as a one-sided *tartine* made with a large, single slice of bread from a round loaf. I'd like to tell you the secret to Au Général La Fayette's first-rate version is the ½ cup of beer, which does give the cheese topping an extra tang. But its superiority depends mostly on the quality of the ham and the bread. While many cafés use the country sourdough loaves from the famous Poilâne and even advertise the fact in their windows as an indicator of overall quality, La Fayette uses a crusty, Auvergne-style French country bread. To make a *croque madame*, top a *monsieur* with a fried egg.

3 tablespoons unsalted butter

⅓ cup flour

2¼ cups milk

Salt and freshly ground black pepper

Pinch of ground nutmeg

2 cups (about ¾ pound) grated Gruyère or Swiss cheese

½ cup light-colored beer

4 slices French country bread (large round loaf)

4 slices ham

1. Make a Mornay sauce. Melt the butter in a saucepan over low heat. Add the flour and mix briskly with a whisk for 2 minutes.

2. Still over low heat, add 2 cups of the milk, continuing to mix briskly with the whisk. When the sauce comes to a boil, season with salt, pepper, and nutmeg.

3. Add ½ cup of the Gruyère to complete the Mornay, remove from the heat, and let cool.

4. Combine the remaining ¼ cup of milk and the beer in a bowl. Add the remaining Gruyère to this liquid, let soak 2 minutes, and drain.

5. Lay a slice of ham on each slice of bread and top liberally with the Mornay sauce, sprinkle with the soaked Gruyère, and cook in a toaster oven or under a broiler until golden brown.

FOUQUET'S

99, AVENUE DES CHAMPS-ÉLYSÉES
TEL: 01 47 23 70 60
MÉTRO: GEORGE-V

The diminished glamour of Fouquet's, the most famous café on Paris's most famous thoroughfare, does not eliminate the singular thrill of crossing under the same red awning that was rolled out for the most famous luminaries of modern times. Architecture and food did not make Fouquet's a historical monument, but celebrity and pizzazz did. Its sidewalk observation deck has viewed in a continuous close-up the passing of the twentieth century.

Nowadays, the only sure way of spotting showbiz celebs in the main dining room refurbished during the 1950s in cherrywood and marble is to look at its new fresco depicting two thousand dignitaries and movie stars bunched outside the café for a class photo. Look, there's Fred Astaire and Ginger Rogers dancing atop the red awning. Yet for all its painstaking detail, the fresco slights one aspect of the café's mystique as it glorifies another. "I lost the movement," concedes its painter, Jean-Louis Pan.

Indeed, the café thrives as a meeting of movements as long as a parade from the Arc de Triomphe to place de la Concorde, as short as a browse across the column width of the *International Herald-Tribune,* or as big and swift as the right hand of general manager Joel Minot as it's extended to a habitué long in years and money. Upper-class Parisians oblivious to the tourists sipping beverages outside still regard the interior terraces, handsome bar, and upstairs dining rooms as if they were the facilities of a private club. The waiters, always cordial, well-mannered, and at your side a second before you need them, encourage this perception.

"It's not a place for food," says Cartier CEO Alain-Dominique Perrin, who's lunched on the avenue George V side of the terrace for over thirty years. "It's a place you like to be to meet friends. It's an institution and it's very friendly."

Fouquet's history as a restaurant started humbly at the turn of the century, with Louis Fouquet cooking on a small grill in the middle of the dining room, and reached its peak in 1938 when the kitchen and its chef, Gabriel Gaubert, were awarded three Michelin stars. Gaubert's signature dish during his thirty-five-year reign was *sole marinette,* a classic of poached fillets of sole coated in egg-Gruyère-Parmesan-béchamel paste, dipped in Villeroy sauce, and fried. Villeroy sauce (I was hoping you wouldn't ask) is an allemande sauce thinned with ham stock and truffle or mushroom stock. Allemande sauce is a reduced velouté sauce thickened with eggs. A velouté, the mother sauce, is a creamy white sauce made with veal or chicken stock thickened with a butter-and-flour roux. A roux . . .

More recently, Fouquet's menu has had an overreaching, overpriced reputation that current chef Bernard Leprince has been unable to surmount. I suppose it's okay for such basics as steak tartare, mackerel poached in white wine, and grilled fish. The *hachis parmentier* (shepherd's pie) is yummy comfort food. But who needs to pay 130 francs (over $20) for a steak tartare when they can watch a century pass before their eyes for the price of a *café crème?*

SHEPHERD'S PIE

HACHIS PARMENTIER

Hachis parmentier, the French counterpart to shepherd's pie, is a hash traditionally prepared by home cooks with the leftover boiled meats from *pot-au-feu* (page 97). Fouquet's serves its *hachis* with a green salad.

MAKES 4 SERVINGS

PREPARATION TIME: 15 MINUTES

COOKING TIME: 1 HOUR

½ cup (1 stick) unsalted butter

1 onion, chopped

½ clove garlic, crushed

1 pound finely chopped cooked beef

2 tablespoons tomato paste

1 cup beef stock

1 bouquet garni (thyme, parsley, bay leaf)

Salt and freshly ground black pepper

3 pounds potatoes, peeled and cubed

1 cup milk

½ cup grated Gruyère cheese

1. Preheat the oven to 375°F.

2. Heat 3 tablespoons of the butter in a large saucepan over medium-high heat, add the chopped onion and garlic, and cook until the onion is soft but not brown, 6 to 8 minutes. Add the chopped meat, tomato paste, and stock and mix well with a spatula.

3. Add the bouquet garni, season with salt and pepper, lower the heat, and simmer gently for 30 minutes. Remove the bouquet garni. Set the meat aside and keep warm.

4. Meanwhile, in a separate saucepan cover the potatoes in cold salted water, bring to a boil, and cook for 20 minutes. Drain the potatoes and mash them with a potato masher.

5. Heat the milk and gradually mix it into the still-hot potatoes. Mix in 2 tablespoons of the butter and season with salt and pepper to taste.

6. Butter a large baking dish with some of the remaining butter and spread half the potatoes on the bottom. Top with the chopped meat mixture and then the remaining mashed potatoes. Sprinkle with the grated Gruyère and dot with the remainder of the butter cut into tiny cubes.

7. Bake in the oven for 10 to 15 minutes and serve immediately.

ROAST LEG OF LAMB
WITH FLAGEOLET BEANS

Gigot d'Agneau aux Flageolets

In the signature dish of Balzar that is also, according to opinion polls, the most popular main course in France, roast leg of lamb is paired with *flageolets*—small, tender French kidney beans that are pale greenish in color. If you can't find dried *flageolets*, substitute your favorite dried white beans.

1. Drain the soaked beans and place them in a large pot with the bouquet garni, carrot, and onion. Cover with the 3 quarts cold water, bring to a boil, reduce the heat to low, and simmer for 2 to 2½ hours, or until the beans are thoroughly cooked. Set aside.

2. Bring the 2 quarts salted water to a boil, add the green beans, and cook about 15 minutes, or until crisp-cooked. Drain and refresh under cold running water. Set aside.

3. Preheat the oven to 450°F.

4. Poke the leg of lamb with the tip of a knife in several spots and insert the garlic slivers. Season with salt and pepper.

5. Make a bed of the onion and carrots on the bottom of a roasting pan. Place the leg of lamb on the vegetables and place in the oven.

6. Reduce the oven heat to 350°F and roast for about 1 hour 20 minutes for a rare roast (about 165°F internal temperature) and up to 2 hours for a well-done roast (175° to 180°F internal temperature).

continued

MAKES 6 SERVINGS

PREPARATION TIME
(AFTER 12 HOURS SOAKING
THE BEANS): 25 MINUTES

COOKING TIME: 3½ TO 4½ HOURS

FOR THE BEANS
1 pound flageolets, *rinsed, picked over, and soaked overnight*

1 bouquet garni (thyme, parsley, bay leaf)

1 carrot, peeled and sliced

1 onion, poked with 4 cloves

3 quarts cold water

2 quarts salted water

1 pound green beans, washed and trimmed

FOR THE LEG OF LAMB
One 4-pound leg of lamb

2 cloves garlic, cut into slivers

Salt and freshly ground black pepper

1 onion, sliced

3 carrots, peeled and sliced

1 cup dry white wine (such as Mâcon)

2 cups water

Salt and freshly ground black pepper

1 tablespoon butter

7. Remove the leg of lamb and add the white wine and water to the roasting pan, mixing well to remove the caramelized juices from the bottom of the pan. Strain through a fine sieve and season to taste with salt and pepper.

8. Reheat and season the beans with salt and pepper.

9. Reheat the green beans in a skillet with a little butter. Season with salt and pepper.

10. Carve the leg of lamb. Place the slices on a large platter on a bed of white beans surrounded by green beans. Douse with some sauce and serve the remaining sauce on the side.

LE VIADUC CAFÉ

43, AVENUE DAUMESNIL
TEL: 01 44 74 70 70
MÉTRO: GARE DE LYON

The avenue Daumesnil viaduct, which carried trains on the Bastille–La Varenne–Saint-Hilaire line for 116 years, now supports Paris's newest grand promenade, Le Viaduc des Arts. The tracks have been replaced by a garden-lined bike/footpath. The stone arcades below house a long row of design galleries and workshops. Naturally, there's a café.

Opened in the spring of 1996, Shake-spearean actor Jean-Baptiste Aubertin's contemporary café wants to prove that modern and chic can also be warm and cuddly. The handsome bar/lounge and dining room are outfitted somewhat stiffly with sofas, homey plaid fabrics, and a tall palm tree. The slatted-teak deck chairs on the delightful sidewalk terrace are shaded by red-canvas canopies. None of this quite fulfills the make-yourself-at-home promise of an old oak cabinet stocked with table linens, sugar bowls, and Aubertin's old record library. Anyone may flip through the library's jazz, Latin, and French-variety sections and pick out something they want to hear. I'd pick out a hit single by a *yé-yé* (1960s French pop) singer, if only to put a smile on Aubertin's face.

Chef Jean-Michel Calvert's menu reflects the postmodern character of the decor. For every Mediterranean fashion (carpaccio, taboulleh, *tagliarini* with tomato and basil, swordfish grilled *à la plancha*) there is a hearty French classic (sautéed rib steak in herb butter sauce, veal kidneys, duck breast, crème brûlée). His most successful dishes boldly incorporate fresh herbs or fruit and vegetable confits: fricassee of chicken with lemon and lime confit as a main course, peach soup with berries and fresh mint for dessert.

Weekend strolls along Le Viaduc des Arts are already a Parisian habit. And so too is its café's American-style brunch featuring orange juice, scrambled eggs, smoked salmon, and, when the Latin jazz band is on break, Sylvie Vartan's French version of an American golden oldie, "Le Loco-motion."

LE VIADUC CAFÉ: Fricassee of Chicken with Lemon and Lime Confit *(page 78)*, Peach and Nectarine Soup with a Sauce of Red Berries and Fresh Mint *(page 158)*

FRICASSEE OF CHICKEN
WITH LEMON AND LIME CONFIT

Fricassée de Poulet aux Citrons Confit

Less sweet and more sour than most of our lemon chicken memories, this summer dish is particularly refreshing served cold the following day.

1. Preheat the oven to 425°F.

2. Wash the lemons and limes and peel only two of the lemons and one of the limes. Cut both the peeled and unpeeled lemons and limes into ¼-inch slices. Cut the slices into cubes. Set aside.

3. Brown the chicken in a mixture of the oil and 1 tablespoon of the butter in a skillet over high heat, 8 to 10 minutes. Add salt, pepper, and the brown sugar and mix well. Remove from the heat and set aside.

4. In a skillet over medium heat, cook the shallots in the remaining butter until soft but not brown, 3 to 5 minutes.

5. Place the chicken pieces in a roasting dish with the lemons, limes, shallots, cilantro, thyme, bay leaf, garlic, and ginger. Mix well. Add the lemon juice and water.

6. Roast for 20 to 25 minutes.

7. Remove the chicken pieces and ½ the garniture and keep warm.

8. Pour the sauce with the remaining garniture into a saucepan and cook over high heat until reduced by half, 7 to 10 minutes.

9. Transfer the sauce to a food processor and process until smooth. Strain through a fine sieve, pressing well to extract all the juices. Adjust the seasoning.

10. Arrange the chicken pieces and reserved garniture on a serving platter, pour the sauce over it, and serve with rice and vegetables.

MAKES 4 SERVINGS

PREPARATION TIME:
30 MINUTES

COOKING TIME: 40 MINUTES

4 lemons

3 limes

1 large chicken (about 2½ pounds), cut into 8 pieces

1 tablespoon vegetable oil

2 tablespoons unsalted butter

Salt and freshly ground black pepper

½ cup firmly packed light brown sugar

5 shallots, minced

1 tablespoon fresh cilantro, finely chopped

2 branches fresh thyme, or 1 teaspoon dried

1 bay leaf

3 cloves garlic, minced

3 tablespoons minced fresh ginger

Juice of 2 lemons

1 cup water

LE RENDEZ-VOUS DES QUAIS

10, QUAI DE LA SEINE
TEL: 01 40 37 02 81
MÉTRO: STALINGRAD

An 1880 waterfront warehouse that might have been the secluded setting for a breezy, laid-back café has been inflicted with the severest of panic disorders. Opened in the fall of 1996 to help revive the area just north of place de Stalingrad and Canal St-Martin, Le Rendez-vous des Quais is under the same ownership and reconfigured roof as the 14 Juillet sur Seine, a new cineplex with six screens and up to a thousand seats to empty and refill around 10 o'clock each night. The turnover throws the café into turmoil as diners with tickets for the later screenings hurry out and moviegoers leaving the prior shows rush in.

The considerable talents of chef/manager Bruno Neveu have done nothing to alleviate these anxiety attacks. If anything, they've extended and exacerbated them. Instead of instituting an efficient menu limited to sandwiches, pre-fab microwavables, and a plat du jour or two, the former pastry chef at the Hôtel Ritz's cooking school has invented a sophisticated café cuisine he describes as—get this!—"like the Ritz but very simple and fast." Moreover, he fully expects his movie-house food to stand up to cheeses brought in from Marie-Anne Cantin, one of the great *fromagers* in Paris, as well as wines expertly chosen with few nods to practicality by filmmaker Claude Chabrol. So ambitious a concept might appear ill-conceived in the calmest of venues. In this cineplex with a complex, it's a recipe for disaster, albeit one that, for as long as it's playing, is not to be missed!

Neveu's nouveau-bistro repertoire consists of authentic dishes done simply, quickly, and with an original twist. In a mixed green salad, goat cheese is melted not over toast, as is customary, but rather in teardrop-shaped bonbons of crisp filo. Shavings of foie gras are served over *mâche* (soft-leaved lamb's lettuce) perfumed with grilled hazelnuts. A *tartine* made with Poilâne bread is topped with sliced bananas and Roquefort cheese, then set under the broiler.

Main courses, even limiting the discussion to seafood, are all the more impressive. Pan-fried cod encrusted in Tunisian *brick* is paired with asparagus cooked in an anise-butter *badiane* sauce. Sautéed *vivaneau* (a sea bream) gets an

79

inlay of chorizo sausage and is served on a bed of ratatouille with a red pepper coulis. Fillet of *rascasse* (scorpion fish) is baked *en papillote* (in a pouch) with a red Saumur wine and butter sauce. And all this comes from a master of pastries who prepares some of the best 30-franc (about $5) desserts in Paris: apricot tart with almond-milk sorbet; kiwi and orange soup scented with mint; macaroon mousseline with pistachios and raspberry coulis; a *nage* (or soup) of strawberries steeped in anisette and orange juice and garnished with raspberries, blackberries, red currants, and fresh mint.

The menu, structured with multiple choices for a variety of start times, includes matching main course/wine/coffee trios for 70 to 80 francs ($12 to $13.50), snacks, homemade ice creams, a *"menu enfant,"* and a *"menu ciné"* consisting of salad, a main course, a glass of wine, and a cup of coffee plus admission to a movie for 135 francs (about $23). The something-for-everyone idea is extended to a beverage assortment offering four coffee blends, five fresh fruit juices, five mineral waters, ten liqueurs, eleven brandies, twelve beers, twelve wines by the glass, and fifteen teas.

The irony, happily lost on the frazzled Monsieur Neveu, is that Le Rendez-vous des Quais might flourish, as it appears to be doing, with little more to drink than the usual blend of arabica and robusta coffee beans caffeinating most café-restaurants. Its vast covered terrace, with metal chairs resting on wood planks inspired by the boardwalk of Deauville, faces a glorious pedestrian mall that runs along the Bassin de la Villette. Its facade bears a montage of movie quotes conceived by graphic artist Claude Maggiori. The glass-fronted interior, with wood chairs and shutters and a sloping concrete ceiling, suggests the setting for the barge navigating the basin connecting Canal St-Martin and Canal de l'Ourcq as much as the seventh—and intermittently most tumultuous—of a cineplex's daily entertainments.

LE RENDEZ-VOUS DES QUAIS: Cauliflower au Gratin *(page 38)*, Chorizo-Scaled Fish Fillets with Ratatouille and Red Pepper Coulis *(page 81)*, Strawberry Soup *(page 161)*

CHORIZO-SCALED FISH FILLETS
WITH RATATOUILLE
AND RED PEPPER COULIS

FILETS DE POISSON EN ÉCAILLES DE CHORIZO
À LA RATATOUILLE ET COULIS DE POIVRON ROUGE

Scaling fish with spicy chorizo sausage is a new fusion concept practiced by a few top French chefs. Through trickle-down gastronomics, Bruno Neveu prepares his café version with vivaneau, a sea bream-like fish from the Indian Ocean, and an elegant ratatouille with vegetables cut into matchsticks. You will also get good results using perch, but I found the sufficiently firm, white flesh of black sea bass to be an ideal substitute. The recipe, with its neatly overlapping cooking steps, is marvelously efficient.

1. Preheat the oven to 400°F.

2. Cut the butter into small chunks and heat to a boil in a saucepan over medium heat. Remove from the heat. When the bubbling noise quiets, strain immediately through a fine strainer to catch the residue of milk solids.

3. Season the fish with salt and pepper. Lay the fillets skin side down, top each with a layer of chorizo slices, and brush with the clarified butter to lacquer the chorizo to the fish. Refrigerate for at least 30 minutes.

4. Meanwhile, prepare the ratatouille. Cut the ½ red pepper and the green pepper, eggplant, and zucchini into thick matchsticks about 2 inches long by ¼ inch wide.

MAKES 4 SERVINGS

PREPARATION TIME:
20 MINUTES

COOKING TIME: 1 HOUR

½ cup (1 stick) unsalted butter

4 fish (about ½ pound each), skin on

Salt and freshly ground pepper

1 pound chorizo sausage, cut into slices a little over ¼-inch thick

2½ red bell peppers, seeds removed

½ green bell pepper, seeds removed

1 small eggplant

3 small zucchini

¼ cup plus 1 teaspoon olive oil

1 large onion, thinly sliced

4 small tomatoes

3 cloves garlic, minced

1 bouquet garni (parsley, thyme, bay leaf), chopped

Parsley for garnish

continued

5. Heat 2 tablespoons of the olive oil in an oven-proof casserole over medium heat and lightly cook the onion and red and green peppers until browned, 10 to 15 minutes.

6. Heat 2 more tablespoons olive oil in a saucepan and cook the eggplant sticks until soft but not brown, 5 to 7 minutes. Remove the eggplant and add to the peppers and onions. Repeat the procedure with the zucchini.

7. Submerge the tomatoes in boiling water for 30 seconds so the skins loosen, peel them with a sharp knife, cut into quarters, and add to the casserole along with garlic, bouquet garni, salt, and pepper. Cover and cook the ratatouille in the oven for 30 minutes. Remove the bouquet garni before serving.

8. Heat a skillet over medium-high heat and cook the fish fillets, chorizo side down, to lightly brown the chorizo, 3 to 4 minutes. Transfer the fish to a baking dish, skin side down, replacing any chorizo slices that may fall off. Cook in the oven for about 15 minutes.

9. Meanwhile, make the coulis. Dice the 2 remaining red peppers and cook in salted boiling water until softened, about 15 minutes. Drain the peppers, transfer to a food processor, add a teaspoon of olive oil, and puree until smooth.

10. To serve, arrange a bed of ratatouille on 4 plates, top each with a fish fillet, chorizo side up, garnish with parsley, and, using a spoon, decorate each plate with a circle of red pepper coulis.

CAFÉ BEAUBOURG

100, RUE ST-MARTIN
TEL: 01 48 87 63 96
MÉTRO: HÔTEL-DE-VILLE

A 16-franc (about $3) espresso is, in many Parisian minds, a *scandale*. But to Café Beaubourg's owner, Gilbert Costes, and perhaps also to its willing habitués, the pricey coffee is an invisible screen that shields the funky caned armchairs on its wide-open terrace from the rowdy ramblers and revelers swarming the vicinity of the Pompidou Center. It could even be regarded as, if not a bargain, a very small premium to pay for the rental of prime café real estate with lots of air space. Café Beaubourg offers its tenants cool detachment from the masses in a serene habitat where artists, designers, trendies, bookish professionals, and intellectual foreigners can hang out or, better still, hang low.

Where these individuals arbitrarily choose to seat themselves is a function of the café's extraordinary geography. In a starkly modern interior hidden behind an old facade, architect Christian de Portzamparc loosely divided the lofty space into smaller sections, employing tall rounded columns, varied seating arrangements, the graceful central staircase, and the elegant footbridge connecting the north and south balconies as subtle barriers. For reasons I'm sure de Portzamparc would find difficult to explain, most habitués prefer to sit in the smaller area to the left (maybe to be near the kitchen and newspaper rack) while newcomers and nonregulars are drawn to the right (perhaps by the New Age dessert displays), unless they seek the privacy upstairs or the absolute lack of it outside on the terrace. What's significant is not so much where you end up sitting as your very freedom to consider the alternatives, ultimately stake out a place of your own, and stay put for as long and as often as you please—the solitary cafégoer's magnificent prerogative. Nearly everyone gets to stretch out in one of the architect's "Bandar Logs," those cumbersome but comfortable designer armchairs instantly identifiable by the curvy, upper-lip-like outline of their backs.

Only the straight-backed young waiters are forbidden to stick to a preferred location. Manager Alain Boudou rotates his crew's positioning, since habitués rarely change theirs, to keep the wordplay between garçon and client fresh. Should a regular favor a particular server—perhaps the communicative Étienne, the prepossessing Stéphane, or the highly stylized Laurent—he too may have to rotate his café geography.

The brasserie (continuous service) menu debuted with the café in 1987 and soon became the prototype for the modern, fashionable, costly café. Its selection encompasses cultural opposites: *croque monsieur* and club sandwich, steak tartare and American hamburger, beef carpaccio and Serrano ham, *mousse aux deux chocolats* and chocolate brownie, *café crème* and cappuccino. I like it best for salads, notably chicken curry and tomato mozzarella, the salmon tartare with a creamy, dill-accented *fromage blanc* sauce, the good *croque monsieur* on Poilâne bread, assorted desserts, situational snacks, and brunch. But conventional dining with unexceptional main courses priced from 70 to 120 francs (about $12 to $20) forms an invisible barrier not worth crossing.

MAIN DISHES

SALMON TARTARE

TARTARE DE SAUMON

Salmon tartare—a dish of chopped raw salmon seasoned here with onion and dill—is a refreshing and light alternative to the ground beef standard, but it does require that you have confidence in your fishmonger and the freshness and high quality of his raw salmon. It is also essential that you work on clean surfaces with clean bowls and utensils.

1. Put the salmon, gravlax, onion, and dill in a large bowl and combine without mashing. Sprinkle lightly with salt and pepper, cover, and chill in the refrigerator for 30 minutes to set in the flavors.

2. Put the *fromage blanc,* the reserved teaspoon dill, and the cucumber, Tabasco, salt, and pepper in a food processor and puree until smooth. Correct the seasoning, adding more Tabasco if you'd prefer the sauce to be spicier.

3. To serve, fill the first of 4 ramekins with ¼ of the tartare, pack it down, but don't mash it, with the back of a spoon, turn the ramekin over a dinner plate, and carefully lift up the ramekin, tapping the bottom if necessary, to unmold. Surround the salmon with ¼ of the sauce. Repeat with the remaining ramekins.

MAKES 4 SERVINGS

PREPARATION TIME:
15 MINUTES
(INCLUDING 30 MINUTES
REFRIGERATION)

1¼ *pounds salmon fillet (skin off), finely chopped*

¼ *pound gravlax, finely chopped*

1 *small-to-medium red onion, minced*

½ *bunch fresh dill, minced (reserve 1 teaspoon for the sauce)*

Salt and freshly ground black pepper

¾ *cup* fromage blanc *or yogurt cheese (see Note, page 21)*

½ *cucumber, peeled and chopped*

A dash of Tabasco sauce

CAFÉ BLANC

40, RUE FRANÇOIS-1ᴱᴿ

TEL: 01 53 67 30 13

MÉTRO: FRANKLIN-D.-ROOSEVELT

In 1965, designers André and Coqueline Courrèges raised the eyebrows and hemlines of Paris fashion by opening, one block from the Champs-Élysées, the icily modern, all-white boutique where they introduced the miniskirt. "Couture Future," their influential *prêt-à-porter* line, was marked by flat-heeled boots, trousers matched with tunic tops, and trapeze-shaped dresses that exposed the knees while effacing the hips.

Thirty years later, their daughter Marie redefined the Paris lunch by opening an all-white café/takeout and rolling out the most radical sandwich formation of the decade, foie gras on a toasted poppyseed bagel. Her ground-breaking *prêt-à-manger* line, arranged on plates with care and flair, also features goat cheese, pastrami, or smoked salmon on a bagel, vegetable tarts, specialty lasagnas, crepes, salads, Brie melted over boiled potatoes, fruit crumbles, and fruit *clafoutis* (pancake-batter tarts). (Marie's full Christian name is Marie-Clafoutis. Really.) For quick weekday lunches, the bagels, though too heavy for *petit déjeuner*, were promptly viewed as *de rigueur* by fashion-hungry shoppers and saleswomen from nearby boutiques (Chanel, Dior, Nina Ricci, and, right next door, Courrèges) as well as employees from—among several media giants with offices in the area—Disney.

Marie, the fashion-hating rebel in the house of Courrèges, was a jockey and equestrian who as a teenager prepared and sold crepes at horse shows. At the age of twenty-four she opened her alternative to—as she describes them—smoky, dirty cafés patronized by crude taxi drivers. The store has the sleek, antiseptic appearance of a cosmetics counter, only the greeting from either Marie, who's fluent in American English, or her engaging manager, Stephanie, is warmer and less intimidating. At the foot of a winding staircase that, by design, gives those below a good view of the bare legs that climb it, is a cozy lunchroom furnished with boxy-cushioned Plexiglas chairs. Upstairs, the white marble floor and Corian countertops are kept spotless.

"White is easy to clean because you know where the dirt is," explains Marie. "My parents believed it's always nice to have white. It's clean. People bring the color."

Putting French attitude on a bagel was part of an overall plan to democratize Courrèges's pricey image. But the hole in the bagel strategy surfaced when journalists ridiculed the trendy café. One writer even inflated the price of a bagel to 60 francs (about $10) when the most expensive variety, with two thick slices of good-quality foie gras and a nice mixed green salad, costs only 44 francs (about $7.30). No one bothered to praise that particular bagel design, so I will. I love it. It's a superb bread texture and shape for foie gras, which ain't chopped liver.

"It's Courrèges," says Marie, railing at the injustice, "and they can't admit that it can be affordable and practical. They forget. My dad invented ready-to-wear. He has stuff that's washable."

FOIE GRAS BAGELS

For total Courrèges correctness, the foie gras bagel might be outfitted, as it is at the boutique's Café Blanc, with a salad of greenleaf lettuce, radicchio, grapefruit sections, tomato, and vinaigrette (page 42).

1. Lightly toast the bagels.

2. Carefully cut the foie gras into slices a little more than ¼ inch thick, delicately lay them atop each bagel half, and serve.

MAKES 4 SERVINGS

PREPARATION TIME:
2 MINUTES

COOKING TIME: 2 MINUTES

4 bagels (preferably poppyseed), sliced in half

12 ounces foie gras

OMELET OF FINE HERBS AND GARLIC

OMELETTE "CÉSAR"

This pancake-style omelet is named for French sculptor and Le Sélect habitué César Baldaccini (usually just "César"), its fine herbs and garlic honoring the Marseille-born artist's Provençal roots. The omelet requires no flipping or folding.

1. Melt the butter in a 7-inch omelet pan over medium heat until bubbling but not brown, about 1 minute.

2. Beat together the eggs, chives, parsley, garlic, salt, and pepper, pour into the pan, and cook on one side only until the top of the omelet is mostly dry and pale pink in color, about 5 minutes.

3. Slide onto a plate, garnish with olives, and serve with slices of baguette or toast.

MAKES 1 SERVING

PREPARATION TIME:
5 MINUTES

COOKING TIME: 5 MINUTES

1 tablespoon unsalted butter

3 eggs

2 teaspoons chopped chives

1 teaspoon chopped fresh parsley

1 clove garlic, crushed

Salt and freshly ground black pepper

Black olives such as Nyons or Niçoise

Baguette slices or toast

SOLE MEUNIÈRE

A simple and classic manner of preparing fish, *à la meunière* consists of fillets or small whole fish that are pan-fried in butter and then sprinkled with browned butter and lemon juice. If using whole sole, as suggested below, ask your fishmonger to gut and scale the fish. If substituting fillets of sole, cook them for about two minutes on each side. La Coupole serves each portion with three small boiled potatoes (*à l'anglaise*).

1. Preheat the oven to 350°F.

2. Heat 1 tablespoon of the butter and 1 tablespoon of the oil in a skillet over medium heat.

3. Rinse and dry the soles and season them with salt and pepper.

4. Coat two of the fish on both sides in flour, and lay them in the skillet, light-skinned side down. Cook 3 to 4 minutes, turn, and cook an additional 3 to 4 minutes. Drain on a paper towel. Place them on a baking sheet in the oven to keep them hot.

5. Repeat steps 4 and 5 with the remaining fish.

6. Drain away the cooking grease, clean the skillet, and melt the remaining butter in the skillet over medium-high heat. When the butter begins to brown, add the lemon juice, stir for a few seconds, and then drizzle over the soles.

MAKES 4 SERVINGS

PREPARATION TIME:
5 MINUTES

COOKING TIME: 10 MINUTES

6 tablespoons unsalted butter

2 tablespoons vegetable oil

4 whole soles (about ½ pound each) or substitute 4 fillets

Salt and freshly ground black pepper

½ cup flour

Juice of ½ lemon

BRASSERIE LIPP

151, BOULEVARD ST-GERMAIN
TEL: 01 45 48 53 91
MÉTRO: ST-GERMAIN-DES-PRÉS

That the Paris intelligentsia was saddened by the death in 1987 of Roger Cazes should come as no surprise. For twenty-one years, Lipp's beloved *limonadier* commanded the legendary brasserie from his "podium" at the foot of its winding stairway with the dictatorial artistry of a great maestro. But who could not also feel sympathy for his nephew and successor, Michel-Jacques Perrochon, when disbelieving diners reacted to Cazes's absence with indignation?

"I tried explaining to them that he had passed away," recalls Perrochon, "and that there was nothing I could do." His apologetic response,

though delivered with the balanced acidity of a fine Chablis, only confirmed an opinion soon shared by Perrochon himself. He just didn't have the stomach for these confrontations. With Cazes there was never an explanation. It was either *oui* or *non*. Perrochon eventually appointed three full-time maître d's to manage the responsibilities his uncle handled alone.

The role men like Roger Cazes and his father, Marcellin, played in establishing and maintaining Paris's great literary haunts cannot be overstated. Although writers like Verlaine, Proust, Gide, and Hemingway made Lipp famous beyond the political world, it was the personal character of *l'accueil*—the reception—they received that made them feel welcome and brought them back. When Hemingway the American drove by in a jeep soon after the liberation of Paris to check on the health of his favorite cognac, Marcellin Cazes the Auvergnat poured him a glass from a rare bottle he had hidden away from the Germans for this very possibility. Hemingway emptied the glass and departed.

Even today, accommodating the dignitaries who flow through Lipp's revolving door requires a diplomat with a memory for faces and a familiarity with the people in the news. These notables generally don't wear name tags. Many insist on sitting at the twenty-five-seat banquette along the left-hand wall, a tough juggling act for a maître d' accommodating up to eight hundred people on a busy Saturday. Few wish to be led upstairs, which despite—or perhaps because of—protestations to the contrary, is

89

Lipp's Siberia. So as not to snub a Nobel Laureate or seat a fascist next to a Communist, ex-waiter and now maître d' Patrick Desaunay, the first third of Cazes's replacement corps, pores over three morning newspapers during his 11 A.M. pre-lunch lunch to prepare for the midday service. If a celebrity surfaces in the dailies to promote a new movie, a new companion, or a new haircut, they're also apt to make an appearance at Lipp, and Desaunay must be ready to satisfy all their special desires short of a Coca-Cola.

The house ban on Coke, long one of Cazes's loudest *nons,* coupled with the "NO SALAD AS A MEAL" warning printed in English atop the otherwise French menu, may give the impression that Lipp is hostile to Americans. The truth is, management is annoyed mostly by those of us who come in wearing baseball hats and jogging suits. Though Lipp is indeed a café restaurant, with unclothed tables reserved throughout the day for beverage service, it does not like to be taken casually. Foreigners are expected to dress not as if they're on vacation but rather as if they're on view, which, when seated below the beveled mirrors, they are.

Those mirrors and the gorgeous Léon Fargue ceramics surrounding them predate by six years Marcellin Cazes's purchase of the brasserie in 1920. The original bright green color of the African-themed mural, now stained tobacco-brown, may be viewed in a tiny section shielded under the stairway from over eighty years of cigarette smoke. The tanned color of the menu card, itself a trademarked classic, is by design. The old house standbys—asparagus vinaigrette, *cervelas* (a pork sausage) *rémoulade,* Bismarck herring, steak and salmon tartare, *choucroute,* roast chicken, *baba au rhum*—are printed in red to tell diners' eyes where to stop. Despite some good daily specials, these are the dishes to order.

Lipp's small terrace has never achieved anything near the wild popularity of its famous neighbors on the opposite side of boulevard St-Germain, Café de Flore and Aux Deux Magots. That's probably due to a questionable decision made by the original owner, Léonard Lipp. In 1880, the Alsatian opened the brasserie that would immortalize his name in a sun-starved space facing north instead of one with southern exposure.

"In Paris there are more bad-weather days than good-weather days," says Perrochon. "This isn't Africa or San Diego, where people hide from the sun."

PORK WITH RED CABBAGE

PALETTE AUX CHOUX ROUGE

Palette refers to the shoulder butt, a juicy and tender cut of pork extending from the shoulder to the shin. The red cabbage balances the aromatic braised pork with its pronounced sourness. Note that preparation begins the day before.

1. *The day before you're going to serve,* in a mortar, crush the garlic cloves with the thyme, paprika, salt, and pepper and add 4 tablespoons of the oil to make a thick spread.

2. Cut small slits in the pork and insert the rosemary leaves.

3. Rub the pork with the spice and oil spread. Place on a dish, cover with plastic wrap, and refrigerate for at least 12 hours.

4. *The following day,* preheat the oven to 400°F.

5. Bring a large pot of water to a boil. Add the cabbage and bring back to a boil. Drain and rinse immediately under cold water. Drain again. Put the cabbage in a large bowl, add the vinegar and the sugar, and mix.

6. Heat the remaining tablespoon of oil in a heavy-bottomed pan over low heat. Add the shallots and onion and cook until wilted, about 5 minutes. Add the blanched cabbage along with the juice it has given off. Over high heat, boil a few minutes, until no liquid remains.

7. Add the cinnamon, nutmeg, cloves, apple, red wine, and vegetable broth. Cover and simmer 45 minutes. Stir occasionally, adding water if the cabbage begins to stick to the pan.

8. Meanwhile, heat a Dutch oven over high heat until very hot and brown the pork on all sides, 3 or 4 minutes on each side, making

MAKES 6 SERVINGS

PREPARATION TIME (AFTER AT LEAST 12 HOURS MARINATION): 30 MINUTES

COOKING TIME:
1 HOUR 15 MINUTES

3 cloves garlic

1 teaspoon fresh thyme leaves

1 teaspoon sweet paprika

1/2 teaspoon salt

1/8 teaspoon freshly ground black pepper

5 tablespoons vegetable oil

3 pounds pork, shoulder butt or Boston butt

10 to 12 leaves fresh rosemary

2 pounds red cabbage, finely sliced

6 tablespoons sherry vinegar

2 teaspoons sugar

2 shallots, sliced

1 onion, sliced

1 teaspoon ground cinnamon

1 teaspoon ground nutmeg

1/2 teaspoon ground cloves

1 apple, peeled, cored, and quartered

sure to seal the edges. Add the ¾ cup water, scraping the pan well to loosen the caramelized juices. Cover and braise in the oven for 1 hour, adding a little more water if it all evaporates.

9. Meanwhile, cut a ¼-inch slash in the flat side of each chestnut, place them on a baking sheet, and cook at 400°F until they start to blister, about 10 minutes. (They can go into the oven with the pork.) Remove the shells and fibrous brown membranes.

10. When the cabbage has cooked 45 minutes, add the chestnuts and cook another 15 minutes uncovered, or until no liquid remains. Season with salt and pepper.

11. When the pork is done, remove it from the Dutch oven, pour off the grease, and add ¾ cup water. Scrape the pan well to remove the caramelized juices. Boil and strain through a fine sieve.

12. Slice the meat. Place the cabbage onto a platter and arrange the slices on top. Spoon a little sauce over the pork and cabbage and serve the rest of the sauce on the side.

¾ cup red wine (such as Bordeaux, Burgundy)

⅓ cup vegetable broth, or water

¾ cup water

10 ounces chestnuts

¾ cup water

CHEZ GLADINES

30, RUE DES CINQ-DIAMANTS

TEL: 01 45 80 70 10

MÉTRO: CORVISART. PLACE-D'ITALIE

In the bars and bistros of La Butte-aux-Cailles, an old hilltop village of small houses and cobblestone streets near place d'Italie, you may to this day listen to incredible tales of the American who ordered the "Cinq-Diamants" salad at Chez Gladines merely as a lunch appetizer and not as an entire meal. According to lore, the shameless glutton emptied the foot-deep bowl of chicken livers and gizzards, tomatoes, eggs, three cheeses, and sautéed potatoes drenched in goose fat, and then, during the same seating, conquered an entire baguette, a full serving of tuna *basquaise,* a certain quantity of Cahors wine, rice pudding, and coffee. But the story, despite its smidgen of truth, is a gross exaggeration. I only ate three quarters of that baguette.

In 1991, there were just a few eateries in this extraordinary and, at the time, quiet neighborhood when Michel Olaizola turned an old corner *bougnat* with tobacco-stained walls and Deco friezes into a café featuring huge portions of Basque food. Today Chez Gladines is one of a dozen or so spots that has made La Butte-aux-Cailles a preferred nighttime destination for young professionals and college-age nomads of the latest social, artistic, and political bents. It is not the finest place to eat in the area, but seated at its communal tables, you do get a good taste of the community—and lots of decent food— for the money. Chef Emmanuel Laisney, though not a Basque native (Olaizola is), does well enough with standards such as *pipérade* (scrambled eggs with tomatoes, peppers, and onions, and ham), tuna, chicken, or tripe *basquaise* (also with tomatoes, peppers, onions), and *patates*— those crisp, goose-fatty potatoes that show up everywhere. Salads are typically ordered for dinner in lieu of an appetizer, a main course, a dessert, and the next day's breakfast.

My memorable lunch debut notwithstanding, there is another Chez Gladines tale, or, more accurately, detail, that made a much stronger impression on me. I was seated across from a ragged-looking young man dressed in the threadbare wool sweater he'd probably been wearing all winter long and watched him put on his eyeglasses for the sole purpose of sampling an unremarkable glass of red wine. Why? you ask. This unlikely connoisseur of café pleasures understood that the critical first contact with a wine, as with an alluring stranger, is made with the eye—preferably a clear-sighted one. Bravo, *monsieur!*

BASQUE-STYLE SCRAMBLED EGGS

PIPÉRADE

This Basque specialty consists of scrambled eggs garnished with tomatoes, peppers, onions, and a slice of ham. The same *basquaise* garnish may be prepared in advance and used for chicken and fish. Chez Gladines serves its *pipérade* with *patates sautées*—potatoes pan-fried in duck fat and seasoned with garlic and parsley.

1. Heat the olive oil in a large saucepan over medium-high heat. Add the garlic and onions and cook, stirring, until translucent, about 8 minutes.

2. Add the chopped tomatoes, green and red peppers, cayenne pepper, white wine, and sugar. Season with salt and pepper to taste, reduce the heat to low, and cook gently, stirring occasionally, for 35 minutes.

3. Heat the butter in a skillet over medium-high heat. Pour in the beaten eggs, season with salt and pepper, and stir with a fork until they are cooked through. Remove from the heat.

4. In a nonstick pan over medium heat, brown the ham slices lightly on both sides, about 3 minutes on each side.

5. To serve, combine the scrambled eggs with the pepper and onion mixture and top each serving with a slice of ham.

Note: To peel tomatoes, place in boiling water for 30 seconds, plunge into cold water, and peel with a sharp knife.

MAKES 6 SERVINGS

PREPARATION TIME:
15 MINUTES

COOKING TIME: 50 MINUTES

2 tablespoons olive oil

2 cloves garlic, chopped

3 onions, chopped

2 tomatoes, peeled and chopped (see Note)

2 green peppers, thinly sliced

1 red pepper, thinly sliced

A dash of cayenne pepper

1/2 cup white wine (such as Bordeaux blanc, Mâcon)

1 tablespoon sugar

Salt and freshly ground black pepper

1 tablespoon unsalted butter

9 eggs, beaten

6 slices ham

SALAD OF WARM SALMON AND MIXED GREENS

SALADE DE SAUMON TIÈDE

Salmon *unilatéral* (a crusty-skinned fillet seared on the one side only) is a 1990s Paris passion. Here it is served in strips over a mixed green salad with sherry vinaigrette—a wonderfully satisfying main-course salad thrown together in 15 minutes tops.

1. Thoroughly wash and dry the salad greens, cut or tear them into 1-inch pieces, and put them in a large bowl.

2. Combine 6 tablespoons of the olive oil, 2 tablespoons of the sherry vinegar, and the lemon juice, salt, and pepper in a small bowl and whisk well. Toss with the salad greens and transfer onto 6 dinner plates.

3. Heat the remaining tablespoon olive oil in a nonstick skillet over very high heat. Season the salmon slices with salt and pepper and cook them skin side down, without turning, until they're brown and crusty on the bottom and most of the top has turned pale pink, 3 to 4 minutes. Remove the salmon from the pan.

4. Add the shallots to the pan, and then deglaze the pan with the remaining 2 tablespoons of sherry vinegar.

5. Turn the slices of salmon over each individual salad so that the browned sides are facing up. Top the salad with the juices from the pan and serve immediately.

MAKES 6 SERVINGS

PREPARATION TIME:
10 MINUTES

COOKING TIME: 5 MINUTES

1 small head Romaine lettuce

1 head frisée

1 bunch watercress

1 head radicchio

7 tablespoons extra-virgin olive oil

1/4 cup sherry vinegar

Juice of 1 lemon

Salt and freshly ground black pepper

1 1/4 pounds salmon fillet, cut crosswise into 3/4-inch slices

2 shallots, minced

BRASSERIE STELLA

133, AVENUE VICTOR-HUGO
TEL: 01 47 27 60 54
MÉTRO: VICTOR-HUGO

The sentimental tone the Right Bank bourgeois reserves for the pronunciation of "Stella" suggests a wistfulness for a long-lost love from a bygone era. But there's neither a woman nor a long history to this love story. The name comes from the Latin word for "star" and is inspired by the Paris square that takes after one. The neighborly "old-fashioned" brasserie situated on one of the three avenues radiating from the place de l'Étoile (star) through the tony sixteenth arrondissement did not assume its adored name, shape, and élan until 1970. For the greater part of the next two decades, weekend lunches at Stella were de rigueur for a generation of privilege.

Regardless, the nostalgic tone is surely one of romantic separation tinged with regret. Stella has not been the same since its owner, Jean Guer-

let, fell ill. Its less than faithful habitués too have changed, not entirely for the better. The brasserie's traditional menu of shellfish from the raw bar, tripe, *choucroute*, and mixed-to-order tartares, its 1970s hotel-coffee-shop-like decor (wood paneling, burgundy drapes, indirect neon lighting, glitzy chandeliers), and the whole business of spending Sundays with the entire family have become outmoded. The hot brunch place in the quarter is an overpriced, American-style luncheonette packed with Parisians who've replaced the René Lacoste alligators on their designer sport shirts with Ralph Lauren polo players.

But not all is lost. As Alex Nubarr arrives for Sunday lunch with his wife, Isabelle, and their fifteen-year-old son, Thomas (their daughter, Lisa, is home studying for an exam), the tiny terrace at the tip of the triangular brasserie is already filled with regulars in amusingly ostentatious poses or get-ups. Inside, Madame Guerlet greets the Nubarrs with a warm smile from her cashier's post at the rear of the bar where the habitués are sipping aperitifs. Quickly they are whisked away to a favorite seating location in the rear where they are treated to team service, with several waiters catering to their every wish. Alex and Isabelle came often as a young couple. Their first apartment was close by. Having moved to another part of town, they return now and then *en famille*—with their kids and their dog.

"We come because we know the people," says Alex. "It's the kindness that matters more than the food." "Many of the couples we know are separating, but we're still together," adds Isabelle. "For us, Stella is from the time we were young and very much in love."

POT-AU-FEU

In the hearty classic "pot on the fire," nothing is wasted. The boiled beef is not lost on the bouillon and vice versa. To honor this spirit, any leftover meat may be used to prepare *hachis parmentier*—Shepherd's Pie (page 74). The bouillon may later be incorporated in any recipe where beef stock is called for, including Poached Eggs in Aspic (page 4). Note that the beef is boiled a day ahead.

1. *The day before you're going to serve,* tie each cut of beef into a compact shape. Place in a large stockpot and add the water. Over high heat, bring to a simmer. Remove the scum that rises to the surface.

2. Add the onion, bouquet garni, tomatoes, and a generous teaspoon of sea salt. Cook over low heat at a very slight simmer for 3 hours.

3. Allow to cool and refrigerate overnight.

4. *The following day,* remove the coagulated fat from the top of the bouillon. Heat slowly in a pot over low heat.

5. Add the carrots, turnips, and leeks to the bouillon. Add water to cover if necessary. Bring to a simmer and cook over a very low heat for ½ hour.

6. Wrap the marrow bones in cheesecloth and tie with a string. Add the parceled marrow bones to the bouillon and simmer for another ½ hour.

7. Remove the meat, vegetables, and marrow bones, and set aside. Remove bouquet garni.

8. Strain the bouillon through a fine sieve lined with a double layer of cheesecloth.

MAKES 6 SERVINGS

PREPARATION TIME (AFTER 12 HOURS BOILING AND REFRIGERATING THE BEEF): 25 MINUTES

COOKING TIME: 4 HOURS 30 MINUTES

4 pounds beef (preferably such cuts as rump roast, bottom round, and pot roast)

3 quarts water

1 onion, peeled

1 bouquet garni (thyme, bay leaf, parsley)

3 tomatoes, cut in half

Coarse sea salt or kosher salt

5 carrots, peeled

3 turnips, peeled

3 leeks, white part only, washed and tied into a bundle

3 slices marrow bone

1 baguette, sliced and toasted

Freshly ground black pepper

Gherkins

Mustard

continued

97

9. Remove as much fat as possible from the broth by placing paper towels on the top and gathering them up as they get saturated with grease. Salt the broth to taste.

10. Remove the marrow from the bones and spread on the toasted bread.

11. Arrange the meat and vegetables in a serving dish, and pour about ½ cup broth over them. Serve with sea salt, freshly ground pepper, gherkins, mustard, and the marrow toasts.

FILLET OF TROUT WITH OLIVE OIL-CREAMED POTATOES

FILET DE TRUITE SUR CRÈME DE POMMES DE TERRE À L'HUILE D'OLIVE

In an ensemble piece of childlike simplicity, the pink fillets of salmon trout sit between golden cushions of olive-oil-and-butter-creamed potatoes too fast and loose to be described as mashed. Though the recipe serves four, I wouldn't anticipate leftovers even after doubling the suggested quantity of creamed potatoes.

1. Cook the potato cubes in a pot of boiling salted water until they begin to soften, about 20 minutes. Drain, transfer to a baking dish, and place in a warm oven to dry, about 5 minutes.

2. Heat the light cream, butter, 6 tablespoons of the olive oil, and the saffron in a double boiler over medium-high heat, stirring occasionally with a wooden spoon, until fully blended.

3. Pass the potatoes through a potato ricer, add them to the butter–olive oil mixture, and stir with a wooden spoon until smooth.

4. Season the trout fillets with salt and pepper, brush on both sides with the remaining olive oil, and cook in a nonstick frying pan over medium-high heat, turning once, for about 2 minutes on each side.

5. Place the trout fillets on the centers of four dinner plates, spoon some potato on both sides of the fillets, and garnish with slices of tomato and lemon.

MAKES 4 SERVINGS

PREPARATION TIME:
10 MINUTES

COOKING TIME: 35 MINUTES

1 pound potatoes (Idaho russet or Yukon Gold), peeled and cubed

2 tablespoons light cream

3 tablespoons unsalted butter

½ cup extra-virgin olive oil

A pinch of saffron

4 salmon trout fillets, 5 to 6 ounces each (substitute trout fillets)

Salt and freshly ground black pepper

½ lemon

½ tomato

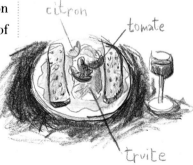

99

Au Roi du Café

59, RUE LECOURBE

TEL: 47 34 48 50

MÉTRO: SÈVRES-LECOURBE, VOLONTAIRES

The history of our dear friend Au Roi du Café—"To the King of Coffee"—at the congenial corner of rue Lecourbe (the curve) and rue des Volontaires (of the volunteers) mirrors the evolution of the Parisian bistro and goes back almost as far. It was opened in 1898 as a retail store selling coal and later wines and liquors. It served both as a café counter and billiards bar, but did not become a full-service eatery until 1989, the year Monsieur Garriq, a coffee salesman, introduced the then-abandoned site to his friends Geneviève and Frédéric Gueze. The young couple toiled for three weeks stripping multiple layers of yellow paint off their new (albeit ninety-one-year-old) baby, and unearthed, to their astonishment and the 15th arrondissement's delight, a small masterpiece of Art Deco design. The unmasked walls of both the front bar section and the rear billiards room (now dining room) were adorned with twenty-seven geometrical friezes in richly colored floral motifs. Decorative glass panels Lalique would have admired divided the front and back sections.

Yet I cherish most the contemporary designs of the owners. Theirs is an authentic, distinctly local Parisian café—the majority of the clients live or work within a five-block radius—that nevertheless embraces tourists and foreigners. Appropriately, the offices of UNESCO can be seen through the elegant, wood-encased front windows.

As a thirty-one-year-old boss, Gueze plays the roles of appreciative kid brother, adored older brother, dutiful son, or grandson-made-good for a coterie of characters who, like Monsieur Hadidi, the eighty-seven-year-old retired boxing referee in a padded-shoulder sports jacket and dark sunglasses, appear as though they've responded to a casting call for "Paris Bistro: The Motion Picture." You can pick out the regulars among the construction workers, grad students, bureaucrats, and entrepreneurs approaching the counter by how they don't order their beverages. Gueze knows what they drink and serves it to them seconds after they've walked in. Should the habitué want to change his customary order, he must instantly alert the barman with a quick "Oh-oh!" and a wave of the hand.

How many visits does it take to establish oneself as a regular of the café? Three, five, maybe not even ten times if you're a foreigner? Gueze says twice and backs it up. During my second visit, he recalled my initial encounter and apologized on behalf of a waiter for having kept a friend of mine waiting for a potato omelet. This is never supposed to happen in Paris!

The basic menu consists of composed salads, steaks, omelets, and three seasonal plats du jour. Didier Vets, from Chinon—better known for its red wines than its chefs—in the Loire Valley, can make the routine seem a little special. His Auvergne-style Stuffed Cabbage filled with sausage, onion, garlic, and carrots is solid com-

fort food that's nearly light and fragrant enough to consume during warm-weather months. Even so, Au Roi du Café is most impressive for its selection of coffees. Gueze grinds four different roasts—Costa Rican, Colombian, Italian, and a house blend—only one of which is supplied by the salesman without whom this café would never have been possible. To Monsieur Garriq's further dismay, Gueze recommends the Italian blend by the famous Trieste roaster Illycaffe over his own.

"That's business," says Gueze. "What else can you do when your café has a name like ours?"

AUVERGNE-STYLE STUFFED CABBAGE

Chou Farci Auvergnat

What makes this stuffed cabbage "Auvergne-style" is the Auvergne sausages normally used in its stuffing. But you can make do with sausages of another origin and keep the name.

1. Preheat the oven to 400°F.

2. Cook the cabbage in salted boiling water to cover for 10 minutes.

3. Meanwhile, finely chop 1 of the onions and 1 of the carrots and combine in a large bowl with the sausage, garlic, parsley, salt, and pepper. Mix well.

4. Drain the cabbage and, when cool enough to handle, separate the leaves. Divide the stuffing mixture into four parts, shape each quarter into a ball, and wrap each ball completely with a cabbage leaf.

5. Dice the remaining onion and carrot and spread them out on the bottom of a baking pan. Drizzle with the vegetable oil, top with the stuffed cabbage bundles, and cook in the oven for 30 minutes.

6. Remove the stuffed cabbage bundles, pour the wine over the onion and carrot, and cook in the oven until the liquid is reduced by half, about 1 minute. Add the water and reduce by half once more.

7. Strain the sauce and pass with the stuffed cabbage.

MAKES 4 SERVINGS

PREPARATION TIME:
10 MINUTES

COOKING TIME: 45 MINUTES

1 small green cabbage

2 medium onions

2 carrots

½ pound ground sausage

1 clove garlic, minced

2 teaspoons chopped fresh parsley

Salt and freshly ground black pepper

1 tablespoon vegetable oil

½ cup dry white wine (such as Mâcon)

1 cup water

GOLDEN SEA SCALLOPS WITH BRAISED LEEKS, CREAM, AND FRESH HERBS

NOIX DE SAINT-JACQUES DORÉES,

ÉTUVÉE DE POIREAUX À LA CRÈME ET AUX HERBES

Pan-frying on one side only produces golden scallops that, just at the point of losing their translucency on the uncooked side, melt in your mouth. The soft, creamy leeks don't go down too badly either.

1. Cut the leeks lengthwise in 4 strips from top to bottom, then slice crosswise to achieve nearly square, ½-inch pieces. Wash the chopped leeks in water three times and rinse well.

2. Heat 3 tablespoons of the butter in a nonstick frying pan over high heat and cook the leeks to set in the color, about 1 minute. Season with salt, pepper, and curry powder, and then let any residual water evaporate over high heat, 2 to 3 minutes.

3. Pour the cream over the leeks and cook, maintaining the liquid at the boiling point and stirring and tasting from time to time, until the leeks have a melt-in-your-mouth consistency, about 10 minutes. Add the chives, and set aside and keep warm.

4. Meanwhile, heat the remaining 2 tablespoons of butter in two separate frying pans, 1 tablespoon per pan, over medium-high heat. Divide the scallops between the pans and cook on one side only until the bottoms are golden, 2 to 3 minutes.

5. Immediately before serving, add the lemon juice and olive oil to the leeks.

6. Arrange 5 or 6 scallops in a circle on each plate, golden side up, and, with a slotted spoon, place a small mound of leeks in the center. Pour the sauce over the leeks, scallops, and plate.

MAKES 6 SERVINGS

PREPARATION TIME:
15 MINUTES

COOKING TIME: 15 MINUTES

2 pounds leeks (about 3 large leeks), white parts only

5 tablespoons unsalted butter

Salt and freshly ground black pepper

Pinch of curry powder

1½ cups heavy cream

1 bunch chives, chopped

30 to 36 sea scallops (about 2 pounds), rinsed and dried on linen or paper towels

Juice of 1 lemon

¼ cup olive oil

La Poule au Pot

121, rue de l'Université
Tel: 01 47 05 16 36
Métro: Alma-Marceau

Much as I pleaded, chef Jacques Dumond was willing to share with me but one of the two family recipes indispensable to this café-bistro since 1970, when his parents chose the name La Poule au Pot. He gave me detailed instructions for his delicately perfumed rendition of the namesake dish ("chicken in the pot"), but wouldn't divulge the formula for the homemade, all-natural cleanser he uses to clean the polished copper casseroles in which it is served. With up to twenty or more shrewd diners requesting *poule au pot*, any chef in his place who couldn't depend on either recipe would surely be in the soup.

As it happens, Dumond has managed to stay above the soup for most of his life. He was raised in an apartment over the café and stayed there long after the La Poule au Pot was leased to outside tenants. As a teenager, he would help his father in the kitchen, chopping the leeks for the chicken broth but never the shallots for the stuffing. ("I wasn't very good at shallots," he recalls.) He didn't assume his father's position until the age of twenty-eight, when his sister and brother-in-law, Stephanie and Patrick Blondeau, took back the management into family hands in 1997.

Situated on a quiet corner near the American Church of Paris and a block from Petrossian, the gourmet boutique where the religion is caviar, the café is instantly recognizable from the green-and-white-striped awning that shades its small terrace. Inside, floral-patterned wall fabrics and antique moldings and light fixtures evoke La Belle Époque. The handsome, dark oak furnishings date back to 1906. A table beside the bar is topped with flowers and newspapers, inviting locals in for coffee or tea during the café's poetically somber afternoons. Office workers, lawyers, and politicians make up much of the lunch crowd. At dinner they are replaced by people who live nearby as well as out-of-towners, who may order from a menu consisting of hearty regional meat and game dishes or the *formule* (daily "formula" or special), offering one of four main courses along with an appetizer or a dessert (not both) for 98 francs (about $16).

Terrific tarts and crumbles should not tempt you to sample anything made from a certain doughlike mixture with the color and consistency of pancake batter. It contains unspecified quantities of flour, egg whites, sea salt, and vinegar and should be used only to clean copper.

CHICKEN IN THE POT

Poule au Pot

King Henri IV became France's first nutrition guru when he decreed that every French family should have a chicken in the pot on Sundays. American families wishing to follow his advice can do so a little more quickly by cooking the broth for a half hour and then adding the chicken directly instead of making the broth the day before. Simmer 1 hour, remove the chicken and strain the broth, return the chicken to the broth, and proceed as indicated below.

1. *The day before you're going to serve,* clean the chicken and remove the wishbone. Refrigerate the chicken.

2. Combine chicken giblets, wishbone, beef bone or knuckle, and veal shank in a large stockpot. Add the water, bring to a boil, and skim off the impurities that rise to the surface.

3. Add the remaining broth ingredients and simmer for 1½ hours. Strain the broth, spoon off any grease that rises to the surface, cool, and refrigerate.

4. *The following day,* combine all the stuffing ingredients in a bowl and mix well. Stuff the chicken and sew closed. Truss the chicken.

5. Remove the hardened fat from the broth. Bring to a boil and add the chicken. Reduce the heat to medium-low and simmer 1 hour, frequently skimming off impurities and grease.

6. Add the carrots, turnips, leeks, and celery. Simmer another 30 minutes.

7. Add the potatoes. Simmer 30 minutes. Season the broth to taste with salt and pepper.

MAKES 6 SERVINGS

PREPARATION TIME (AFTER 12 HOURS PREPARING AND REFRIGERATING THE BROTH): 20 MINUTES

COOKING TIME: 3 HOURS 30 MINUTES

One 1½-pound chicken

FOR THE BROTH
1 beef bone or knuckle

1 veal shank

3 quarts water

1 leek, white part only, washed and chopped roughly

1 stalk celery, chopped roughly

1 large onion, peeled and poked with 3 whole cloves

2 carrots, peeled and chopped roughly

FOR THE STUFFING
3½ ounces lean ground pork

2½ ounces pork fat, ground

2 ounces Parma ham, chopped finely

2 slices white bread, crusts removed, crumbled

1 tablespoon sour cream or heavy cream

continued

8. Remove the trussing and place the chicken on a platter, surrounded by the vegetables. Remove the stuffing and carve at the table. Serve with sea salt, gherkins, and mustard. Serve the broth separately.

1 tablespoon finely chopped fresh tarragon leaves

1 shallot, finely chopped

2 cloves garlic, crushed in a garlic press

1 egg, lightly beaten

2 tablespoons finely chopped fresh parsley

Salt and freshly ground black pepper

FOR THE SERVING
VEGETABLES

3 carrots, cut into ¹/₂-inch slices

3 turnips, cup into ¹/₂-inch dice

6 leeks, white part only, washed

6 stalks celery, cut into 2- to 3-inch pieces

4 potatoes, peeled and cut into ¹/₂-inch dice

Salt and freshly ground black pepper

Coarse sea salt or kosher salt

Gherkins

Mustard

Café de la Place

23, RUE D'ODESSA

TEL: 01 42 18 01 55

MÉTRO: MONTPARNASSE-BIENVENUE, EDGAR-QUINET

On a cold afternoon, as biting winds and freezing rain send even Rodin's Burghers of Calais running for cover, a young woman in sunglasses applies sunscreen to her face, neck, and arms. She is seated outdoors on the cobblestone terrace of Café de la Place. Incredibly, she is not alone. Two fifteen P.M. is nearer the beginning than the end of what the Left Bank considers lunchtime and so only one . . . no, I write too fast, none of the café's sixteen al fresco tables is vacant.

For reasons the national weather bureau, Météo France, cannot explain, this Parisian triangle has a microclimate with the predictably sunny forecasts you only find in Mediterranean travel brochures. It must have something to do with the Moroccan oranges and Spanish avoca-

107

dos sold only a few yards ahead at the Edgar-Quinet market. Regardless, were his solar terrace not in such desperate need of summertime shade, proprietor Francis Tafanel could easily replace the great leafy tree out front with a fruit orchard and make a killing on January peaches.

Besides a sun with few vacation days, Tafanel also has working for him a talented young chef, Sabine Cermenati, efficient waiters, a theater-district location sufficiently removed from Montparnasse mob scenes, and a tenant operating one of the city's best crepe stands. His Auvergnat's tale, however, is not rags-to-riches but rather riches-to-riches. His father, Georges, came to Paris after World War II without a centime in his pocket and worked his way up from a waiter to boss in the café division of the Tafanel family's beer-distribution empire. In 1992, as cafés were closing by the dozens, Georges was convinced the traditional café would experience a renaissance and urged his son, then twenty-five, to open such a place. To that end, the café's retro design, with its custom zinc and advertising collectibles, appears a bit calculated. The green-and-beige canvas awning and customized coffee cups and saucers were clearly "inspired" by Café de Flore's and manufactured by the same suppliers.

Yet it is hard to find fault when young Tafanel has backed up his clichéd motto, *Ici, comme à la maison* (Here, like at home), with three honest plats du jour always priced under 60 francs ($10). Insiders know to come on fish Fridays for the likes of *rascasse* (scorpion fish) fillet with a cool *vierge* tomato sauce and boiled pota-toes topped with *fromage blanc* and chives or a trout fillet topped with a cool pepper sauce and sided with celery root puree. The drawback to the specials-only policy is that yearnings for, say, *pintadeau au estragon* (young guinea fowl stuffed with chopped onions and carrots in a tarragon sauce) cannot be satisfied on demand. Furthermore, late diners run the risk of encountering those dreaded wet bistro fingers. Sold-out specials are traditionally erased from slate boards with three fingers and a little saliva. This can be one of the saddest gestures in the French dining experience.

Perhaps fearing disappointment, many rely on Café de la Place only for composed salads, sandwiches, omelets, and ice creams, whose fine quality is no mystery. Tafanel buys his breads from Poilâne, his cheeses from incomparable Boursault (Pierre Vernier's shop is nearby at 71, avenue du Général-Leclerc), and his ice creams from a fellow Auvergnat named Berthillon, widely regarded as the best *glacier* in France.

The superiority of the café's crepes, however, may be as difficult to explain as its exceptional climate. Perhaps they are related. Crepemaker Joseph Karadeniz claims the sole difference is a personal feeling many of his colleagues lack: shame. It is what prevents him from using powdered skim milk, reheating pregrilled crepes, and refilling Nutella jars with a cheaper brand of hazelnut-chocolate spread. Yes, French culture is being threatened by generic Nutella.

CAFÉ DE LA PLACE: Fillet of Sole with Cold Tomato Sauce *(page 109)*, Crepes *(page 164)*

FILLET OF SOLE
WITH COLD TOMATO SAUCE

FILET DE SOLE AU SAUCE VIERGE

Chef Sabine Cermenati's affinity for topping hot with cool turns up on both sides of this delightfully simple spring/summer Friday special. The sole fillets take on a cool *vierge* (virgin) sauce consisting of chopped tomatoes, olive oil, garlic, and basil. The boiled potatoes are garnished with *fromage blanc* and chives.

1. Put the potatoes in a saucepan, cover with cold salted water, bring to a boil, and cook until tender when pierced by a fork, 20 to 25 minutes.

2. Meanwhile, combine the tomatoes, olive oil, vinegar, garlic, and basil in a large bowl, season with salt and pepper, and set aside.

3. About 5 minutes before the potatoes are done, melt 1 tablespoon of the butter in a large nonstick skillet over medium-high heat. Lay 3 of the sole fillets in the pan and cook until golden on the bottom side, about 1½ minutes. Turn, season the golden side with salt and pepper, and cook the other side until golden, about 1½ minutes. Season that side with salt and pepper and transfer to serving plates. Melt the remaining butter in the pan and cook the remaining fillets in the same manner.

4. Drain the potatoes, cut into slices just under ½ inch thick, and divide among 6 dinner plates. Top each serving of potatoes with a tablespoon of *fromage blanc* and sprinkle with chopped chives. Spoon tomato sauce over fish fillets and serve immediately.

MAKES 6 SERVINGS

PREPARATION TIME:
10 MINUTES

COOKING TIME: 30 MINUTES

2 pounds potatoes, peeled

2 pounds tomatoes, halved, seeds removed, and chopped

3 tablespoons extra-virgin olive oil

1 tablespoon red wine vinegar

1 clove garlic, minced

1 tablespoon chopped fresh basil

Salt and freshly ground black pepper

2 tablespoons butter

6 sole fillets, about 2½ pounds

½ cup fromage blanc or yogurt cheese (see Note, page 21)

2 tablespoons chopped chives

LES FONTAINES

9, RUE SOUFFLOT
TEL: 01 43 26 42 80
MÉTRO (RER): LUXEMBOURG

For years, the yellow neon that highlights the hideous 1970s decor of Les Fontaines was valued by possessive habitués mostly because it repelled the unknowing hordes of Parisians and tourists traversing a busy street connecting the Panthéon with the Jardin du Luxembourg. More recently, a coterie of Latin Quarter intellectuals viewed the yellowish glare as an antifashion statement which, by cloaking the very best taste in the very worst taste, separated true aesthetes from their susceptible and superficial counterparts. Today, the tubing's intactness reinforces the reassuring words new chef/proprietor Jean-Marie Plas-Debecker repeats in his café-bistro—and probably in his sleep—nearly every night: "Nothing's changed."

Well, not quite. Plas-Debecker was the hand-picked successor of Roger Lacipière, the Auvergnat chef/proprietor whose gift for procuring only the finest ingredients turned the ugly café into one of Paris's best-valued bistros. For months before his official departure in January 1997, Lacipière towed his thirty-two-year-old apprentice around the kitchen and, more significantly, the marketplace, introducing him to the top purveyors at the Rungis wholesale market and teaching him how to distinguish the very best meats, seafood, and cheeses. During the many late nights and early mornings the two men shopped, cooked, ate, and drank together, the teacher, even when soused, offered not a single word of encouragement to his pupil.

"He never told me he was pleased," says Plas-Debecker, recalling his difficult rite of passage. "They [older Auvergnats] don't say those things. I perceived a satisfaction."

Plas-Debecker, himself a native of Auvergne and a talented chef at that, next set out to win over skeptical diners by retaining the kitchen staff, the food and wine suppliers, and the photocopied hand-written menus favored by his predecessor while slowly introducing new dishes so as not to be noticed. Les Fontaines may still be counted on for outstanding meats and game in colossal quantities. In truth, Plas-Debecker is a marked man who lacks the freedom to offer lesser alternatives. If he didn't buy the best, the purveyors at Rungis would rat on him to the entire Parisian bistro community and, even worse, his mentor. Consequently, there are few better places to dig into veal kidneys *dijonaise*, sweetbreads *forestière*, or simply a steak *au poivre* for under 100 francs (about $16). Composed salads consisting of vegetables, seafood, or the highest-caliber charcuterie are, by themselves, regional feasts. The fillet of St. Pierre (John Dory), a signature fish dish, is still blessed with fifteen spices.

The measure of Plas-Debecker and his wife Josiane's success may be seen in a packed dining room that, as before, compels some to eat standing at the stainless steel bar. Moreover, Lacipière, the old master, comes in for lunch every now and then. And though he doesn't convey his approval with a polite smile or comment, one senses a satisfaction.

LES FONTAINES: Stuffed Artichokes with Ratatouille Niçoise *(page 22)*, Salad of Warm Salmon and Mixed Greens *(page 95)*, Veal Sweetbreads with Wild Mushrooms *(page 111)*, Tarte Tatin *(page 157)*

VEAL SWEETBREADS
WITH WILD MUSHROOMS

RIS DE VEAU FORESTIÈRE

MAKES 6 SERVINGS

PREPARATION TIME (AFTER 4 HOURS FOR SOAKING AND 1 HOUR PRESSING): 40 MINUTES

COOKING TIME: 45 MINUTES

Most of the tripe—or variety meat—dishes routinely served at café-bistros were eliminated from this collection due to their limited availability at American markets and their limited appeal to American tastes. The exception is veal sweetbreads (thymus glands), which the specialized butchers known as *tripiers* prize, along with brains, as the most delicate of variety meats. They must be soaked in cold water for 4 hours to dissolve their bloody patches and soften for easy removal the filaments that cover them. Jean-Marie Plas-Debecker's splendid recipe, portioned, I should warn you, for diners who love sweetbreads, is liberally garnished with earthy wild mushrooms. To obtain the freshest possible sweetbreads, you may need to order them from your butcher in advance.

1. Soak the sweetbreads in the water, with ½ teaspoon vinegar added, for 4 to 5 hours, changing the water and vinegar occasionally, until the sweetbreads whiten and the water is clear. Drain.

2. Put the sweetbreads in a saucepan, cover by 2 inches with cold salted water, and bring slowly to a boil. Reduce the heat to medium-low, let simmer 2 minutes, and drain.

3. Plunge the sweetbreads into cold water and when cool, delicately peel off all the filament you can without tearing the flesh or the connective tissue holding the two sections together. Place the sweetbreads between two towels, top with a weighted board, and leave for 1 hour.

4. Preheat the oven to 325°F.

3 pounds veal sweetbreads

2 to 3 quarts water

2 to 3 teaspoons white wine vinegar

5 tablespoons unsalted butter

½ pound white mushrooms, cleaned and sliced

1 pound assorted wild mushrooms (oyster, chanterelle, porcini, shiitake, morel, cremini), cleaned, and all except the morels sliced

1 onion, minced

1 carrot, diced

1 bouquet garni (parsley, thyme, bay leaf)

Salt and freshly ground black pepper

1 cup dry white wine (such as Mâcon or Sancerre)

1 cup beef stock

1 tablespoon tomato paste

2 tablespoons crème fraîche (page 17), or sour cream

continued

5. Heat 2 tablespoons of the butter in a skillet over medium heat, add the white and wild mushrooms, and cook for 5 minutes. Set aside.

6. Heat 2 tablespoons of the butter in a casserole over low heat and cook the onion and carrot with the bouquet garni, salt, and pepper until tender but not browned, about 10 minutes.

7. Season the sweetbreads with salt and pepper, add to the casserole, and cook gently for 10 minutes, turning over once.

8. Add the mushrooms, cover, and cook for an additional 12 minutes. Add the white wine, beef stock, and tomato paste to the casserole, and transfer to the oven. Cook, basting occasionally, for 25 minutes. Remove the sweetbreads and mushrooms with a slotted spoon and transfer to a serving dish.

9. Place the casserole over high heat, add 2 tablespoons crème fraîche, and boil for 3 minutes. Whisk in the remaining 1 tablespoon butter and cook 1 more minute.

10. Pour the sauce over the sweetbreads and mushrooms, and serve.

CAFÉ VÉRY

JARDIN DES TUILERIES
TEL: 01 47 03 94 84
MÉTRO: TUILERIES

With Paris's largest restaurant developers all submitting proposals for a new food concession in the Jardin des Tuileries, you have to marvel at the foresight of the Grand Louvre Project, overseer of the museum's $1.4 billion renovation, for choosing the most accessible concept from the candidate with the least financial resources. Robert Petit submitted to the curators of original masterpieces what is essentially a faithful copy of his novel menu at Dame Tartine. He lifted the name Véry from an old café in the Tuileries that Josephine Bonaparte had demolished.

The café's modern pavilion and underground kitchen, designed by architect Antoine Stinco, makes for an inconspicuous presence in the northwest corner of the gardens. When trees are in bloom, its glass panels and cherrywood shutters are not visible from thirty-five feet away. Having so discreet a café in so public a place is ideal, Petit noted to me, but surely not to the Louvre's selection committee, for government ministers meeting their mistresses for lunch. In the unlikely event they are spotted by their spouses or other acquaintances, the wide-open location in the middle of a great park visited by thousands gives their secret tryst the illusion of innocence.

In an article published in the daily *Libération* in the summer of 1997, Marc Meneau, the Michelin-three-starred chef at L'Espérance in Burgundy, described the inspiration behind his latest pièce de résistance, a lobster dish in a coconut curry sauce. It recalled the more modest salmon with coconut curry sauce I and many others had sampled a year before, for only 40 francs (about $6.60), at Café Véry. The comparison is made not to diminish Meneau's achievement but to illustrate Petit's: cosmopolitan French cuisine that's easy to like and afford. The salmon plate typifies Petit's knack for contrast: the aggressive, exotic flavor of coconut and curry matched to the more passive and familiar sensations of salmon and zucchini; the creaminess of the sauce set against the silkiness of the fish and the light crunch of the julienned zucchini.

Finding so special a dish in so unassuming a café is ideal for the many discriminating chefs who come to Café Véry on their day off. Its Sunday-in-the-park setting allows them to stretch out, unwind, grab a casual lunch, drink a little too much wine, maybe joke around with friends. But in the likely event they are spotted by colleagues, clients, or food critics, their carefully honed reputations for demanding only the highest-quality food go unchallenged.

SALMON WITH COCONUT MILK

SAUMON AU LAIT DE COCO

The curry flavor in Robert Petit's delightful recipe is gentler than we're used to finding in Thai-influenced recipes. Though I encourage you to leave it as is, you can make it a little spicier by adding more curry powder.

1. Melt 1 tablespoon of the butter in a skillet over low heat. Add the julienned zucchini and the water, cover, and cook until crisp-cooked, 2 to 3 minutes. Drain through a fine sieve, reserving the juice you obtain.

2. Melt 1 tablespoon of the butter in a heavy-bottomed pan over high heat. Add the onion and the zucchini juice and cook until reduced by half, 3 to 4 minutes.

3. Add the heavy cream and the curry powder and cook until reduced by half, about 3 minutes.

4. Add the coconut milk and the basil. Bring to a boil.

5. Meanwhile, mix the cornstarch with the cold water.

6. As soon as the coconut milk mixture comes to a boil, add the cornstarch mixture. Stir and remove from the heat. Once the sauce thickens, adjust the seasonings.

7. Season the salmon well with salt and pepper.

8. Melt the remaining 2 tablespoons of butter in a nonstick skillet over high heat. Cook the salmon slices 1 to 2 minutes on each side.

9. When you are ready to serve, reheat the zucchini and the sauce.

10. To serve, spread the sauce on the bottom of each of 4 plates, distribute the zucchini among the plates, and top with the salmon slices. Serve with lemon.

MAKES 4 SERVINGS

PREPARATION TIME:
10 MINUTES

COOKING TIME: 15 MINUTES

1/4 cup (1/2 stick) unsalted butter

4 zucchini, cut into julienne

1/3 cup water

1 small onion, finely sliced

3/4 cup heavy cream

1 teaspoon curry powder

2/3 cup unsweetened coconut milk

3/4 cup fresh basil, finely chopped

2 teaspoons cornstarch

1 tablespoon cold water

Salt and freshly ground black pepper

1 1/4 pounds fresh salmon fillet, cut into 4 thin slices

1 lemon, quartered

CAFÉ CHARBON

109, RUE OBERKAMPF

TEL: 01 43 57 55 13

MÉTRO: PARMENTIER

The great paradox of the café counterculture concerns what it means to be *branché*, which is to say "hip," or "trendy." Parisians who sacrifice all to be *branché* nevertheless use the word in a pejorative, even damning tone ("I adored the café before it became *branché*" is a fashionably correct if hip-ocritical thing to say). No wonder Olivier, the resourceful creator/manager of the most popular haunt in the new Bohemia centered on rue Oberkampf, denies *branché* was something Café Charbon was ever meant to be.

"I don't like the idea of a *café branché* and I would detest going there," says Olivier. "I don't know how you make a place *branché*. I certainly did not try."

What he did do, working for Jean-Claude Serges, was to convert a lofty 1886 Belle Époque space that housed the *café-théâtre* Le Nouveau Casino, later a café-cinema, and—continuing to reflect the decline of the neighborhood—a metalworks, into a spectacularly grand café that is to Oberkampf's emerging artistic community what the cafés Le Dôme and La Rotonde were, some eighty years prior, to Montparnasse's. The comparison may at first seem ludicrous considering the cosmopolitan modernity the Montparnasse cafés extended to the Left Bank and the lax, secondhand ethos Café Charbon now embraces on the Right Bank. But art scenes must move with—and ahead of—the times. Bourgeoisification, as well as ballooning rents and tourism, has during this century chased Parisian bohemians from Montmartre to Montparnasse to St-Germain-des-Prés to the Bastille to the run-down apartment buildings and warehouses in the northeast villages of Oberkampf, Belleville, and Ménilmontant. And if Café Charbon appears humble, rough-edged, and working-class when compared to its now legendary predecessors, it may just be that, as Olivier says, the starving young artists back then were better off than they are now.

I don't doubt they were better fed. You certainly wouldn't expect much from a kitchen that erased American-style pancakes from its popular brunch menu because they're too difficult to make *à la minute*—at a moment's notice. Furthermore, you can't develop a loyalty to any

115

particular dish or specialty, since the café changes chefs nearly as often as its generously portioned plats du jour ("Claude, the current chef, doesn't have a specialty," Olivier once remarked. "That's his advantage.") While Charbon can surprise you from time to time with a good, low-priced fish special for lunch, most regulars depend on a three-way salad that might include leeks vinaigrette and a salad of mozzarella and tomato.

The wonder of Café Charbon is in the possibility of eating cheaply and modestly—or merely sipping a coffee—in such magnificent surroundings. By removing the partition that separated the former cinema from its café, Olivier has thrown open the high-ceilinged, pillar-free room and its original frescoes and classic backbar. Interestingly, the remainder of the relics are entirely new to the space. By installing a zinc bar, antique mirrors, chandeliers, gas lamps, cozy moleskin banquettes and booths, and assorted bric-a-brac, and choosing a name from the coal-selling cafés of yore, he has reconstructed a circa 1900 bistro that isn't an official historical landmark only because it never existed.

So contrived and faddishly retro a design, however successful its realization, only adds to the skepticism of critics such as Gérard-Georges Lemaire, the author of *Les Cafés Littéraires* (published by Henri Veyrier in 1987), who disparaged the new arty haunts for being too—you guessed it—*branché*. "It's like the nightclubs," he remarked to me, complaining of their short-lived appeal. "Three articles [in newspapers or magazines] and it's finished."

Still, the popularity of Café Charbon, which opened in 1995, shows no sign of fading. The outdoor terrace has been extended to the adjacent sidewalk in front of a hair salon. A more intimate, no-eats spinoff, Café Mercerie, has opened across the street. True, Café Charbon's bar is packed late into the night with young hipsters and witless poseurs who scream at one another over blaring music. But calm afternoons and calmer mornings draw an older crowd (thirty to fifty) of creative professionals for quieter café pleasures.

"I like the morning best," relates Olivier, stuck in anti-*branché* mode. "If I only had the night, I would be miserable."

BLAST-SAUTÉED SARDINES AND TAPENADE

SARDINES À LA PLANCHA ET TAPENADE

Tapenade, the thick Provençal paste of anchovies, capers, black olives, and olive oil that accompanies these fresh sardines, may also be used to garnish Le Café Marly's Tomato and Goat Cheese Cake (page 20). *"A la plancha"* is the Spanish method for grilling seafood "on the griddle."

1. Put the sardines in a bowl and toss with ½ cup of the olive oil. Season with salt and pepper and set aside.

2. To make the tapenade, put 3 tablespoons of the olive oil and the olives, garlic, anchovies, capers, and a few turns of freshly ground pepper in a food processor and process until blended into a fine puree, about 30 seconds. Set aside.

3. Heat a large skillet over high heat until very hot. Sprinkle the bottom of the pan with coarse sea salt. Place 8 to 12 sardines in the pan and cook, depending on their size, for 30 seconds to 1 minute on each side. Repeat with the remaining sardines.

4. Make a bed of tapenade on 6 plates and top each with 6 sardines in a rosettelike pattern. Decorate with a leaf of lettuce and a wedge of lemon and drizzle with a little olive oil.

MAKES 6 SERVINGS

PREPARATION TIME:
10 MINUTES

COOKING TIME: 5 MINUTES

36 fresh sardines (about 3 pounds), gutted and cleaned with heads on

¾ cup extra-virgin olive oil

Salt and freshly ground black pepper

1 pound black olives such as Nyons, niçoise, or Kalamata, pitted

1 clove garlic, crushed

3½ ounces anchovy fillets packed in oil

3 tablespoons drained capers

1 teaspoon coarse sea salt

A handful of soft-leaved green lettuce

1 lemon, cut into 6 wedges

117

VEAL CHOP WITH CARAMELIZED CARROTS AND PEARL ONIONS

Côte de Veau, Sifflets de Carottes Caramelisées aux Petits Oignons

If I had to pick a star of this dish, it would be the caramelized carrots. Their sweet buttery taste, delivered with a sufficiently crunchy texture, makes me dizzy with pleasure. Still, it's hard to say how much staying power this sensation would have were it not offset by the sharper sweetness of the pearl onions and scallions.

1. Slice the carrots on a diagonal bias to produce slabs a little more than ¼ inch in thickness.

2. Melt 4 tablespoons of the butter in a skillet over medium heat, add the carrots, water, and sugar, season with salt and pepper, and cook, stirring occasionally, for 7 minutes.

3. Add the pearl onions and cook for an additional 3 minutes. Set aside and keep warm.

4. Melt 1 tablespoon of the butter in a large skillet over medium heat. Season the veal chops with salt and pepper and cook gently, turning once, until golden brown on both sides, about 10 minutes (6 on the first side, 4 on the second).

5. For the final minute of cooking, add the thyme, bay leaf, garlic, scallions, and remaining 1 tablespoon butter. Deglaze the pan by adding the water.

6. Remove the veal chops and set them on the center of each of 6 dinner plates.

7. Surround each chop with a laurel of carrots and onions, top with pan juices, and serve.

MAKES 6 SERVINGS

PREPARATION TIME:
10 MINUTES

COOKING TIME:
25 TO 35 MINUTES

2 pounds carrots, peeled

6 tablespoons (¾ stick) unsalted butter

1 tablespoon water

5 tablespoons sugar

Salt and freshly ground black pepper

18 to 24 pearl onions (about ¾ pound), peeled and outer layer removed

Six 1-inch-thick veal chops, about ½ pound each

1 sprig fresh thyme, or ½ teaspoon dried

½ bay leaf

1 clove garlic

6 scallions, sliced, green parts only

1 tablespoon water

LE SÉLECT

99, BOULEVARD MONTPARNASSE
TEL: 01 45 48 38 24
MÉTRO: VAVIN

Details of poet Hart Crane's fabled expulsion from the Sélect in July 1929 are, at best, sketchy. According to an English newspaper account, Crane, among the young American writers of the "Lost Generation"—John Dos Passos, Henry Miller, William Faulkner—who chose the Sélect as their Montparnasse base, was arrested after first refusing to pay the full amount of a large bill and subsequently lunging at a policeman's throat. A French historian wrote only that Crane was tossed into the *panier à salade*, which, had these words been employed to indicate, literally, "salad basket," might've mitigated the poet's disgrace through the reward of a free meal—the niçoise salad, perhaps, or the pungent *baltique* (potatoes, onions, tomatoes, hard-boiled egg, and Baltic herrings). But in this instance the term was used as a colloquialism meaning "paddy wagon." Regardless, Crane received a hero's welcome upon his return to the Sélect.

Having only recently seen a drunk forcibly removed from the Sélect, I can say that getting tossed out on your ear isn't what it used to be and thus mock the similarly banal laments romanticizing an era that needs no such embellishment. But at least one nostalgic gripe, that the south-facing terrace is not as sunny as it once was, is entirely justified. In the '80s, an eight-story office building was constructed over the café's across-the-boulevard neighbor, La Coupole, blocking all late-afternoon rays. Yet despite a competitor's

MAIN DISHES

crass act of solar sabotage, the glorious glass-enclosed terrace continues to be both esteemed as a greenhouse for the growth of ideas and relationships and denounced as a poorhouse for the sentimental suckers who shell out 28 francs (nearly $5) for a Coke and 15 francs (about $2.50)—a Montparnasse high—for an espresso.

Moody habitués prefer the interior—a warm, softly lit space of iron-railed moleskin banquettes, dark wood tables, bentwood chairs, and Art Deco moldings and light fixtures that were all part of a stunningly subdued $70,000 renovation. During the quiet before mealtimes, the melancholy ambience consoles your solitude. At noon, when students idling in the back are cleared out to make room for the lunch rush, expert waiters in white double-breasted smoking jackets become visible only in a blur. They are moving away from you even as you order. If you take too long choosing between, say, the omelet of fine herbs or the Welsh rarebit (a café classic for English expats of beer-marinated cheese melted over toast), they're gone before you've decided, purportedly to serve impatient businesspeople who can no longer spare the time for café small talk, relaxation, and, most sadly of all, laziness.

"Money wasn't so important when people seemed to have enough," grumbles Didier, a waiter at the Sélect since 1982. "Now, making money is everything."

That even applies to father-son relationships, especially those within the café trade. Third-generation Auvergnat Michel Plégat did not inherit the Sélect from his self-made father. He bought it, at a

steep price to boot. ("It wasn't a gift," says Plégat, unamused by any discussion of the transaction and unwilling to elaborate on the credit terms.) He did, however, acquire one of the best places to rendezvous—and wait for a companion—in all of Paris. If a friend is going to be late for an appointment (in Left Bank terms, that means a minimum of 45 minutes after the agreed-upon time), he can call the café and have you summoned to the house telephone in the basement. Being paged over the loudspeakers at the Sélect is a thrill every café romantic should experience, even if he has to ring the café himself from the pay phone and sprint back to his table to hear his name called.

"The rendezvous, it's either at my place or at the Sélect," French actor Hippolyte Girardeau wrote in the café's guest book. "There is no other solution."

LE SÉLECT: Omelet of Fine Herbs and Garlic *(page 87)*, Welsh Rarebit *(page 121)*

THE PARIS CAFÉ COOKBOOK

WELSH RAREBIT

This is a classic holdover from the 1920s, when the cafés of Montparnasse served this Welsh specialty to homesick English expats and other foreigners who found the comfort of cheddar cheese melted with beer, flavored with Worcestershire sauce, and served over toast either more appealing or less frightening than French fare. The U.K. counterpart to the French *croque monsieur* (and perhaps also Swiss fondue), and the preferred melted-cheese toast of the Lost Generation, is a scrumptious, home-away-from-home treat.

1. Preheat the broiler.

2. Place the cheddar cheese and beer in a saucepan and heat over low heat until melted, about 10 minutes. Add the Worcestershire sauce and mix well with a wooden spoon.

3. To toast the bread slices with the melted cheese, lay the bread in a baking pan, spoon melted cheese onto each slice, and heat under the broiler until lightly browned, about 1 minute. If some of the melted cheese spills onto the baking pan, so much the better. The resulting burned cheese crisps are, as the British would say, "brilliant."

MAKES 6 SERVINGS

PREPARATION TIME:
2 MINUTES

COOKING TIME: 15 MINUTES

1½ pounds cheddar cheese, grated

¼ cup amber beer

3 tablespoons Worcestershire sauce

6 slices bread from a large round loaf, lightly toasted

ZÉBRA SQUARE

3, PLACE CLÉMENT-ADER
TEL: 01 44 14 91 91
MÉTRO: KENNEDY-RADIO FRANCE

The notion of dressing waitresses in short, furry, zebra-striped dresses came almost as an afterthought to restaurateur Patrick Derderian. His motivation for naming his contemporary café-brasserie Zébra Square originally had nothing to do with a horselike mammal and everything to do with the letter *Z*. Having made his mark with a chain of eateries called L'Amanguier, he aspired to leap the alphabetical gamut of entrepreneurship before his forty-fifth birthday.

Further evidence of his peculiar genius can be seen on the surfaces of a stylishly postmodern café space where Voltaire is quoted on the walls and exactly 101 lamps hang like drops from the ceiling primarily so Derderian can boast they number more than one hundred. His is a mediagenic sensibility easily understood by the mascaraed intellectuals of French radio and television who work next door at the Maison de Radio France. From 8 A.M. coffees to 2 A.M. cocktails, Zébra Square is their rendezvous.

The challenge of modernizing a classic French menu, the downfall of most neo-bistros and neo-brasseries, fell upon chef Patrice Hardy, who succeeded by looking to the Mediterranean rather than California for ideas. (Parisian trendies love to copy Los Angeles or New York cool, but rarely get it right.) His appetizer repertoire includes marinated anchovies, fried calamari, and ricotta ravioli beside traditional escargots and foie gras. As main courses, familiar meat and seafood dishes are paired with risotto, pasta, or basmati rice instead of potatoes. The beef tartare *à la Vénitienne*, one of five varieties, is enhanced with anchovies, basil, and tomato. Fresh herbs and olive oil are a constant presence.

The most appealing desserts, a coffee tart, and a passion fruit soup with pineapple and mango, lack only the concept coordination of the "Zébra Z," a pastry striped with layers of *chocolat noir* and *chocolat blanc*. Oddly, the choice of a dozen desserts that would seem to offer something for everyone has one glaring omission. None begins with the letter *A*.

ZÉBRA SQUARE: Grilled Scallops with Mushroom Risotto *(page 123)*, Coffee Tart *(page 153)*

GRILLED SCALLOPS WITH MUSHROOM RISOTTO

NOIX DE SAINT-JACQUES GRILLÉES, RISOTTO AUX CHAMPIGNONS

The risotto will be a great success with any combination of wild mushrooms: portobello, chanterelle, black trumpet.

1. Cook the mushrooms in 1 tablespoon of the butter in a skillet over medium heat, stirring, until all the liquid is evaporated, about 5 minutes. Add all but 2 tablespoons of the parsley and remove from the heat. Set aside.

2. Heat the olive oil in a saucepan over medium heat, add the onion, and cook until soft but not brown, about 5 minutes.

3. Add the rice and stir for 1 minute.

4. Combine the wine and stock. Add ¼ of the liquid to the rice and cook, stirring frequently, until fully absorbed. Repeat the procedure until no liquid remains.

5. Add 2 tablespoons of the butter and the cream, Parmesan, and cooked mushrooms. Season with salt and pepper. Keep warm.

6. Meanwhile, prepare the grill or preheat the broiler.

7. Season the scallops with salt and pepper.

8. Grill the scallops until just cooked through and opaque, 2 to 3 minutes on each side.

9. In a small saucepan, melt the remaining butter, season with salt and pepper, and add the remaining parsley.

10. Spoon the risotto onto individual plates and surround with scallops. Drizzle the parsley butter over the scallops.

MAKES 4 SERVINGS

PREPARATION TIME:
15 MINUTES

COOKING TIME: 35 MINUTES

10 ounces white mushrooms, cleaned and sliced (5 cups)

7 ounces wild mushrooms, cleaned and sliced (2½ cups)

7 tablespoons unsalted butter

¾ cup finely chopped fresh parsley

2 tablespoons olive oil

1 onion, finely chopped

2 cups Arborio rice

½ cup dry white wine (such as Mâcon, Muscadet)

4 cups fish or vegetable stock

⅓ cup heavy cream

⅔ cup freshly grated Parmesan cheese

Salt and freshly ground black pepper

20 to 25 sea scallops (about 1½ pounds total), rinsed and dried on a linen or paper towel

LA FLÈCHE D'OR CAFÉ

102 BIS, RUE DE BAGNOLET
TEL: 01 43 72 04 23
MÉTRO: ALEXANDRE-DUMAS, PORTE DE BAGNOLET

Amid the jumble of junk, funk, and spunk that animates the remarkable Flèche d'Or Café, no presentation has seemed more startling than a fillet of cod baked *en papillote* with baby vegetables, lemon liquor, cinnamon, and vanilla, a dramatic departure from its more conventional version. It wasn't the particular set of flavors that mattered so much as the very idea of seri-ous food. Once people are programmed to expect the unexpected, be it a Sunday rummage sale and tango ball or a band called Grave de Grave that plays *"rock-folklo-électricogravissime,"* some-thing so familiar as *cuisine française* can appear downright bourgeois. No wonder the café's young French chef has chosen the name of a rev-olutionary. He calls himself Che. Che Salinas.

The Charonne train station on the old Petit Ceinture line sat abandoned and ravaged for sixty-one years before eight artists converted it into what is now a wildly popular café/bar/per-formance space/nightclub. Its tolerant attitude and cover charges elicit a citywide following. Opened in May 1995, La Flèche d'Or is a decon-structed funhouse built around an evolving panoply of junk art. A sculptured train curls over a bar built with the wood ties from the rail-road below. The quieter glassed-in waiting room where lunch and beverages are served overlooks the weed-strewn tracks with the missing beams.

The space, like its large, diverse, and often boisterous clientele, defines itself according to the music it listens to. Techno Tuesdays, funk Thursdays, rock Fridays, French-variety Satur-days. Within that program, Che might have bet-ter luck with empanada Mondays. But to serve Latin American food to this offbeat crowd, he would probably have to change his name to Pierre.

PAPILLOTES OF COD FILLET AND VEGETABLES

Papillotes de Cabillaud et Petits Légumes

A papillote is a pouch in which meats, fish, or vegetables are baked and served. Though an aluminum foil pouch, as suggested here, is probably less attractive and imaginative and certainly less edible than other materials (rice paper, cabbage leaf, banana leaf, etc.), it does make for easy preparation and dramatic presentation.

1. Preheat the oven to 425°F.

2. Cook the green beans, carrots, and turnips in boiling water for 3 minutes, then drain.

3. Combine the mushrooms with the cooked vegetables and make a thin bed of vegetables about the size of a cod fillet on the center of each of 4 sheets of foot-square aluminum foil. The foil should extend at least 4 inches from the vegetable bed on all sides.

4. Top each bed with 1 cod fillet, 1 teaspoon lemon juice, and a pinch of cumin, and season with salt and pepper. Dot with cubes of butter.

5. Pull the borders of foil up gently, and carefully fold the edges tightly. Each papillote must be airtight, with plenty of space left inside.

6. Place the papillotes on a baking sheet and cook, allowing 10 minutes for each inch of the cod's thickness.

7. Transfer the papillotes to dinner plates and serve.

MAKES 4 SERVINGS

PREPARATION TIME:
10 MINUTES

COOKING TIME: 15 MINUTES

½ pound green beans, ends trimmed

¼ pound carrots, peeled and cut into thin sticks

¼ pound turnips, peeled and cut into thin sticks

1½ cups thinly sliced white mushrooms

4 cod fillets, about ½ pound each (or substitute scrod)

4 teaspoons fresh lemon juice

½ teaspoon cumin

Salt and freshly ground black pepper

2 to 4 tablespoons unsalted butter, cut into small cubes

Au Général La Fayette

52, rue La Fayette
Tel: 01 47 70 59 08
Métro: Le Peletier

Named for a solder who took part in three revolutions, two French and one American, Au Général La Fayette made history of its own during the first days of an Irish invasion. With a Belgian in command, the bistro was the first in France to serve Guinness on tap and has long maintained its high standing in the Paris beer subculture with a selection of eleven Belgian, Irish, German, and French drafts. There's beer too, thankfully not stout Guinness, inside the bistro's first-rate *croque monsieur*. The grated Gruyère is presoaked in milk mixed with a light ale before it's melted atop the sandwich.

The bistro's 1886 origins are discernible in its old mosaic floor, mahogany bar and tables, and black sign with gilded letters fixed between two panels of glass. Such "fixed-glass" signage is characteristic of fin-de-siècle storefronts. The caned terrace chairs and trompe l'oeil murals, however, were part of extensive renovations made by current owner Michel Planchon in 1986. Though handsome and true to the original decor, the newer furnishings will require another decade of wear and, yes, tobacco smoke, to look authentic.

Regulars—businesspeople at lunch, younger revelers at night—know to order the foods that go best with beer. That means an emphatic *oui* to excellent charcuterie, composed salads, cheese and smoked fish platters, mackerel and herring fillets, and *choucroute* (especially the pig's knuckles version) and an unequivocal *non* to desserts. However, wine drinkers of varying thirsts are hardly neglected by Planchon, a new-generation Auvergnat who drinks no beer. All his chosen wines are served by the glass, the bottle, and the *fillette*—an antiquated measure that's two-thirds the size of a full bottle.

AU GÉNÉRAL LA FAYETTE: Croque Monsieur *(page 72)*, Sauerkraut with Pork and Sausages *(page 127)*

SAUERKRAUT WITH PORK AND SAUSAGES

Choucroute Garnie

This is the Alsatian classic of braised sauerkraut garnished with sausages, bacon, pork, and smoked goose breast. I've simplified the recipe and adapted the selection of meats to include only those available in American markets. You may substitute your favorite types of sausages and smoked pork.

1. Rinse the sauerkraut in cold water and drain by squeezing it between the palms of your hands.

2. Heat the vegetable oil in a 5-quart casserole or large saucepan over medium heat and cook the onions and apple until the onions are translucent but not colored, about 5 minutes.

3. Add the sauerkraut, salt, beer, wine, and water.

4. Wrap the juniper berries, peppercorns, bay leaves, and fresh thyme in cheesecloth, and add this to the sauerkraut. Lower the heat, cover the saucepan, and cook until the sauerkraut has a melt-in-your-mouth consistency but still retains a touch of crispness, about 1½ hours.

5. After the sauerkraut has cooked ½ hour, add the slab bacon.

6. After an hour, add the frankfurters, bratwurst, and smoked pork chops.

7. Meanwhile, cook the potatoes in boiling salted water until soft, 15 to 20 minutes, and then drain.

8. Remove the cheesecloth sack from the sauerkraut, and correct the seasoning if necessary.

9. Cut the bacon and bratwurst into slices and serve directly from the casserole or in a large serving dish, with the potatoes on the side.

MAKES 6 SERVINGS

PREPARATION TIME:
15 MINUTES

COOKING TIME:
1 HOUR 30 MINUTES

3 pounds sauerkraut

2 tablespoons vegetable oil

4 small-to-medium onions, thinly sliced

1 apple, peeled, cored, and thinly sliced

A pinch of salt

1 cup light beer

1 cup dry white wine (such as Mâcon)

1 cup water

1 tablespoon juniper berries

10 black peppercorns

2 bay leaves

2 branches fresh thyme

1 pound slab bacon (whole)

6 frankfurters (whole)

6 bratwurst (whole)

1 pound smoked boneless pork chops

12 to 18 small new potatoes, peeled

Salt and freshly ground black pepper

127

FISH CHOUCROUTE

CHOUCROUTE DE POISSON

Choucroute prepared with smoked fish, rather than meat, is gaining popularity in Paris, albeit more slowly than you'd expect. The fatty bacon, sausages, and smoked goose breast that would make a traditional *choucroute garnie* nutritionally incorrect in many an American household is not yet so large a concern in France. Brasserie de l'Île St-Louis prepares its fish *choucroute* with smoked haddock (finnan haddie), which is readily available in Paris markets. I've substituted smoked trout, which you have a much better chance of finding in U.S. markets.

1. Rinse the sauerkraut in cold water and drain by squeezing it between the palms of your hands.

2. Heat the vegetable oil in a 5-quart casserole or large saucepan over medium heat and cook the onions until translucent but not colored, about 5 minutes.

3. Add the sauerkraut, a pinch of salt, and the wine and water.

4. Peel off the skin of the trout fillets, cut off the ends of the fillets, and wrap the skins and ends in cheesecloth along with the juniper berries, peppercorns, and bay leaves. Add this to the sauerkraut. Lower the heat, cover the saucepan, and cook until the sauerkraut has a melt-in-your-mouth consistency but still retains a touch of crispness, about 1½ hours.

5. A few minutes before the end of cooking, take 2 cups of liquid from the sauerkraut and bring to a boil over medium-high heat in a saucepan with the trout fillets. Lower the heat, cover, and simmer for 2 to 3 minutes.

MAKES 6 SERVINGS

PREPARATION TIME:
15 MINUTES

COOKING TIME:
1 HOUR 30 MINUTES

3 pounds sauerkraut

2 tablespoons vegetable oil

*4 small-to-medium onions,
    thinly sliced*

Salt

*1 cup dry white wine
    (such as Mâcon)*

1 cup water

*6 smoked trout fillets,
    3 pounds total*

1 tablespoon juniper berries

*1 tablespoon black
    peppercorns*

2 bay leaves

*1 cup crème fraîche
    (page 17), or sour cream*

1 tablespoon chopped chives

*1 tablespoon chopped fresh
    parsley*

6. Place the crème fraîche in a serving bowl and season with the chives and parsley.

7. Remove the cheesecloth sack from the sauerkraut, and correct the seasoning if necessary.

8. Serve the sauerkraut on dinner plates with the smoked trout fillets and a small scoop of the seasoned crème fraîche for dipping the trout.

BAR DE L'ENTRACTE

47, RUE DE MONTPENSIER

TEL: 01 42 97 57 76

MÉTRO: BOURSE, PALAIS-ROYAL

A typical afternoon in a not-so-typical place, the quadrangular dreamscape that is the Palais-Royal. Sommelier Mouss Alrafei sneaks out of his workplace, the majestic dining room of Le Grand Véfour, steps into a tiny casement-windowed café where rue de Montpensier meets rue de Beaujolais, circles behind the bar, pours himself a Whisky-Coca (Scotch and Coke), and snatches a single french fry from an unattended plate. Minutes later, Francis Joffo walks over from Muscade, the *salon de thé* (tea) situated under the palace arcades, and pours himself a glass of red. Outside, actor Eric Heyon parks his scooter and sits down at a lone table on the makeshift terrace for an espresso. This has been his daily routine, rain or shine, 85 degrees or 25 degrees, since he appeared in a play the year prior at the Théâtre Palais-Royal directly across the street.

The scene has not changed all that much since 1862, when Alfred Delvau, author of the guidebook *Cafés & Cabarets de Paris,* praised the café as the preferred haunt of local merchants, theatergoers, and the most famous actors of his day. He didn't much care, though, for the name the dramatis personae had given their watering hole: Café de la Pissotte (a corruption of *pissotière,* meaning public urinal). A more recent and respectful sobriquet, Chez Marcel, survives the reign of Marcel Duveau, the beloved proprietor who retired in the spring of 1997. He was replaced by his low-key employee, Philippe Cassin, who gives regulars—and the photo crews who often shoot fashion spreads out front—the run of the place. The concierge upstairs is less hospitable. During one lazy Sunday brunch, sometime after my orange juice, baguette, confiture, charcuterie, cheese, roasted potatoes, and egg and tomato salad but before my dessert of baked apple and French toast (80 francs—about $14—complete!), I watched him lock a minimally clothed model behind the gate at the foot of the Passage Beaujolais, the stairs climbing to rue Richelieu her only escape.

Weekday lunches and dinners are usually shorter and less eventful. The menu consists of salads, quiches, charcuterie and cheese plates, and cutesy main courses like chicken wings in plum sauce and *parmentière poëlée à la villageoise,* a glorification in words, but not presentation, of panfried potatoes topped with sautéed vegetables. French fries are made exclusively for staffers and, as soon as their heads are turned, the regulars who think they own the place.

FRENCH TOAST

Pain Perdu

ntracte wants its sweet French toast kept simple. Just how simple? When I asked Philippe Cassin if he put some vanilla extract into the eggs, hardly a radical suggestion, the Entracte manager protested. "Our way is *familial*, Daniel," he responded. "No vanilla." Cassin makes *pain perdu* (literally: lost bread) with slices of stale baguette and serves each order with a baked apple. Nice idea! As toppings he proposes honey or jam. Instead of baguette, you may substitute brioche or any day-old bread at your disposal and you can even add a teaspoon of vanilla to the eggs, if you promise not to tell Cassin about it.

1. Put the eggs, milk, and sugar in a bowl and beat with a whisk. Dunk the baguette slices in the egg mixture, turning once, and let them soak.

2. Heat the butter in a large skillet over medium heat. Shake off the excess egg from the bread slices and lay them in the skillet. Immediately reduce the heat and cook until the bottoms are brown, about 2 minutes. Turn and cook until the undersides are brown, about 2 minutes.

3. Put 3 slices on each plate and serve with honey or jam.

MAKES 4 SERVINGS

PREPARATION TIME:
10 MINUTES

COOKING TIME: 5 MINUTES

4 eggs

1 cup milk

½ cup sugar

Twelve 1-inch slices stale baguette (at least a day old)

1 to 2 tablespoons unsalted butter

Honey

Jam

The extent to which France not only tolerates but also protects the needs of its smokers is demonstrated by an obscure law concerning its *tabacs,* the state-controlled tobacconists that, usually doubling as cafés, have a monopoly on the sale of tobacco. Before closing for vacation, a *tabac,* like a pharmacy, must post an announcement in the window with the names and addresses of the nearest *tabacs* lest their habitués endure minutes without their precious smokes. These signs are seldom seen, as *tabacs* rarely close for vacation. Their licensed operators, aside from being frugal workaholics mostly of Auvergnat origin, are probably not too keen on giving their customers the whereabouts of their competitors.

Most tourists will enter a Paris *tabac* only to buy phone cards, stamps, or chewing gum and exit quickly without noticing the flurry of activity at the bar. Only tobacco-fuming foreigners who feel persecuted by their local nonsmoking laws are likely to stick around long enough to appreciate the *tabac* as a hub for continuous comings and goings and the easy exchange of second-hand gossip and smoke. The red *"carotte"* that hangs proudly outside every *tabac* is a long, diamond-shaped beacon granting everyone— even nonsmoking Americans—instant access to the source of Paris's nicotinic, caffeinated pulse.

AUX DEUX MAGOTS

170, BOULEVARD ST-GERMAIN
TEL: 01 45 48 55 25
MÉTRO: ST-GERMAIN-DES-PRÉS

As a pantheon to the legends who rested their elbows, backs, and feet on its polished wood tables, red moleskin banquettes, and mosaic floor, Aux Deux Magots greatly ennobles the ritual in a cup of otherwise ordinary espresso. Paradoxically, current management trivializes the preparation of its expensive ham omelets and salmon quiches. Whereas some cafés find the title *cuisinier* (cook) more appropriate than *chef* for the persons preparing their modest meals, Aux Deux Magots further declasses their status to the rank of *officiers*, meaning those who man its *office*. The word *office* itself downgrades *cuisine* to indicate a service kitchen where no real cooking is done.

Not that Picasso, Hemingway, de Beauvoir, Joyce, Wilde, or the millions following in their eternal wake have ever journeyed to this illustrious corner with real cooking in mind. They've come to express their good taste, not to exercise it. After World War I, poet/critic André Breton and his surrealist cohorts assembled at the table immediately opposite the door so they could ridicule everyone who entered. The few editorialists who still frequent the café exhibit their superiority more discreetly. While American snobs are apt to read *Le Monde,* flaunting their sophistication and, in some instances, their inferiority complex, French show-offs may be seen leafing through the pages of the *International Herald-Tribune*. This angers English-speaking tourists, whose requests for information from *Trib* readers are sometimes met with cold, uncomprehending stares. The unflappable waiters, on the other hand, see nothing unusual in a client who's not fluent in the language of his newspaper or, for that matter, his companion.

Perhaps the only oddity that might startle a white-aproned waiter into spilling an old Grand Champagne Cognac—or, just as tragically, the café's exceptional hot chocolate—would be his spotting a young bohemian under the ornate moldings and crystalline chandeliers of this classic coffeehouse. Even before the tourists and arrivistes of the 1950s and 1960s chased it away, the Deux Magots' artistic community tended to be from the old guard, with younger upstarts preferring its neighbor and rival for over a century, Café de Flore. Nowadays, if a young man seated below those two grotesque Chinese figurines—*magots*—is wearing jewelry, it's most certainly cuff links and not nose rings.

Despite competing loyalties to the Flore or Brasserie Lipp, there's no denying that the Deux Magots' wraparound terrace affords the most resplendent people-watching, sun-worshiping vista on the golden café triangle. And since the others use the word *terrace* to identify their sidewalk appendages, it's appropriate for the Deux Magots to upgrade the status of its ninety-seat, shrub-enclosed extension out onto the square by referring to it as *le jardin*—the garden—of St-Germain-des-Prés.

FRIED EGGS WITH CANADIAN BACON

OEUFS SUR LE PLAT BACON

Nothing too special about this ordinary plate of Canadian bacon and eggs, except that the bacon cooks—and thus drips—its salty, fatty juices over the eggs. Oh, yeah, one other thing. It has been fed to some of the century's greatest writers at one of the world's most celebrated cafés and is thus, as much as croissants and jam, the Paris breakfast of literary champions.

1. Heat the oil in a small skillet over medium-high heat. Crack the eggs into the skillet and reduce the heat.

2. Meanwhile, quickly place the Canadian bacon slices into a microwave and cook on high for 50 seconds (or heat in a skillet over medium heat for 1 minute, turning once). Remove from the microwave, lay the bacon over the eggs, and let cook for about another minute.

3. Slide onto a warm plate and serve with the baguette slices.

MAKES 1 SERVING

PREPARATION TIME:
1 MINUTE

COOKING TIME: 5 MINUTES

2 teaspoons vegetable oil

2 eggs

3 slices Canadian bacon

A few slices of baguette

PAUSE CAFÉ

41, RUE DE CHARONNE
TEL: 01 48 06 80 33
MÉTRO: LEDRU-ROLLIN

The search for a lost cat lures unfamiliar neighbors out of hiding in the 1996 film *Chacun Cherche Son Chat* (released in the United States as *When the Cat's Away*), a delightful portrait of loneliness and coming together in a small district coping uneasily with its sudden resurgence. Director Cédric Klapisch cast Madame Renée Le Calm and the Pause Café as themselves. One's an elderly pet lover baffled by the odd values of the newcomers, some with tattooed and pierced body parts and Day-Glo hair dyes, circulating on the streets outside her apartment; the other, a hip HQ for that emerging counterculture. Much as he's profited from the latter's upbeat portrayal, Didier Alaux would prefer that his café assume the unifying role of Grisgris, the lost cat. As a changing Paris thirsts for the inclusive warmth of a trusted café, a community in constant flux naturally craves its *pause-café*, its "coffee break."

The motorcycles stationed out front and the nouveaux bohemians parked on the terrace's caned aluminum chairs may give passersby the impression of a *café branché* overly impressed with its coolness. But a closer inspection extending beyond the casement windows to the U-shaped bar, old yellow Formica tables, stripped walls, and grotesque chandelier/clock reveals an easygoing atmosphere and a diverse clientele near—but clearly not of—the raucous Bastille quarter. Alaux himself detests the Bastille element and won't venture beyond rue de Charonne, a self-imposed travel restriction typical of Parisians who localize their movements to the small villages within the big city.

The modest but appealing menu of combination platters, composed salads, and homemade *tourtes*—savory, puff-pastry-lidded tarts filled with such couplets as broccoli-cheddar, chicken-curry, and beef-Roquefort—was introduced by Ahsen Ataya, an Algerian singer/guitarist who daylights as a café chef. The popularity of the *tourte*-and-salad lunch has spread itself over the Paris café landscape, irking the man not flattered by his many imitators. "Why can't they come up with their own concept?" protests the ever-grumbling Alaux, as if he himself had invented the *tourte*. "There are still plenty of new things to do."

More difficult to duplicate is the front-porch camaraderie and streetscape view of a community—and century—in transition. When the terrace is full, some resort to taking their beverages on the squat concrete stanchions that block cars from climbing the curb. Others linger on the periphery, listening for the *didididididit* those handheld, wireless credit-card validators set off when processing a payment. (Café aficionados recognize that printing noise as the first reliable indication a table is about to become available.) Their competition for vacancy includes not only those standees waiting alongside them but also sitting habitués who chase the afternoon sunlight across the terrace, zigzagging from table 5 toward table 1 as the sun dips to the west.

"They don't even wait for the tables to be cleared," says Alaux. *C'est chiant!*"—"It's damn annoying!"

One regular who stays loyal to a single table is Madame Renée, now a recognized celebrity to locals as well as French and foreign cinephiles who hunt down this and other Paris cafés featured in their favorite films. Usually she holds court with friends old and new; at other times, a dog is her sole companion.

"Men have let me down," remarks the raspy-voiced Madame Renée in her indelible movie line, "but animals, never!"

BROCCOLI AND CHEDDAR CHEESE TOURTE

TOURTE AU BROCCOLI ET CHEDDAR

Paired with a salad, puffy *tourtes* like this one from Pause Café signal not just an increasingly popular lunch alternative but a complete lifestyle shift on bistro-busy rue de Charonne.

1. Preheat the oven to 400°F.

2. Combine the eggs, heavy cream, and milk in a large bowl and beat with a whisk. Add the broccoli, cheddar cheese, salt, and pepper and stir well.

3. To prepare the *tourte,* roll out ¾ of the puff pastry into a circle ⅛ inch thick. Butter a 9-inch tart pan and line the pan with the dough, leaving ⅓ inch of pastry overlying the edges.

4. Fill the piecrust with the egg, broccoli, and cheese mixture. Turn the overlying edges of pastry onto the filling and brush with some of the egg yolk.

5. Roll out the remaining puff pastry ⅛ inch thick. Cut a circle the size of the tart. Cover the filling. Press the pastry edges down to close well and seal them with egg yolk. Cut a ½-inch hole in the center. Brush the pastry with the remaining egg yolk.

6. Cook 50 minutes on the bottom shelf of the oven. If the pastry begins to brown too much, cover with a piece of aluminum foil.

7. Cool on a rack. Serve warm or cold.

MAKES 6 SERVINGS

PREPARATION TIME:
10 MINUTES (PLUS 4 HOURS
FOR MAKING DOUGH)

COOKING TIME: 50 MINUTES

5 eggs

1½ cups heavy cream

½ cup milk

1½ cups cooked chopped broccoli

1½ cups shredded cheddar cheese

Salt and freshly ground black pepper

2 pounds puff pastry (recipe follows)

Unsalted butter for greasing tart pan

1 egg yolk, beaten

137

PUFF PASTRY

PÂTE FEUILLETÉE

The flaky foundation for countless pastries, tarts, *tourtes,* and sweet and savory delicacies, puff pastry is made by placing a slab of chilled fat (usually butter) between layers of pastry dough (known as the *détrempe*), which is then rolled out and folded over in thirds six to eight times. These repetitions are referred to as "folds." This produces nearly a thousand paper-thin layers which rise up during baking to create a light, crisp, fluffy pastry. It's important that you work fast, that the butter and dough be kept cold and of the same firmness at all times, and that you do the rolling and folding as neatly and precisely as possible. This is facilitated by the fact that this recipe calls for small amounts of dough and *détrempe* that are easy to work with.

1. Cut 2 tablespoons of the butter into small pieces and place in a food processor fitted with a steel blade with 1¼ cups of the flour and the salt. Pulse until the mixture resembles a fine meal, about 20 seconds. With the motor running, pour in the water in an even stream and blend until the dough forms a ball, 20 to 25 seconds (if it doesn't form a dough, add 1 to 2 teaspoons cold water). Remove the dough, dust lightly with flour, wrap in plastic wrap, and refrigerate for 40 minutes.

2. Meanwhile, cut the remaining 12 tablespoons butter into small pieces, place in a large bowl, and toss with remaining ¼ cup flour until fully coated.

3. Transfer to a flat, floured surface and knead the mixture, working the butter and flour with the palms of your hands, to form a rough 4-inch square. Place the square between 2 sheets of waxed paper and, using a rolling pin, flatten to a 4-inch square. Peel off both sheets of waxed paper, dust the butter mixture well with flour,

MAKES ENOUGH DOUGH
FOR ONE 9-INCH TART
(1 POUND OF DOUGH)

PREPARATION TIME:
20 MINUTES (PLUS A
MINIMUM OF 3½ HOURS
TOTAL REFRIGERATION
TIME)

*14 tablespoons (1¾ sticks)
    unsalted butter*

*1½ cups flour (plus extra
    for dusting)*

¼ teaspoon salt

*⅓ cup plus 1 tablespoon
    ice water*

wrap in another sheet of waxed paper, and refrigerate until it has the same consistency as the dough, about 20 minutes.

4. Flour a flat work surface and, using a rolling pin, roll the dough into a 6-inch square. Lay the butter mixture diagonally over the dough so that it appears like a diamond inside the square. Fold over the corners of the dough to enclose the butter and pinch together the seams to seal the dough.

5. Using a rolling pin, roll the dough into a 6 × 10-inch rectangle. Turn the dough and brush off any excess flour. Fold the rectangle in thirds by first folding down the top 6-inch side and then folding up the bottom 6-inch side over the top (you should have 3, equal, overlapping layers). Turn the dough seam side down so that an open edge is facing you. Using a rolling pin, gently press the top and bottom ends of dough. Then roll the dough from the center out, never rolling within ½ inch of the top and bottom ends, to form a 6 × 10-inch rectangle. Fold the dough in thirds again. Wrap in plastic and chill for 40 minutes. This completes two "turns" of rolling out and folding the dough.

6. Unwrap the dough and complete two more turns, always starting with the seam side down, gently pressing the top and bottom ends of the dough, and never rolling within ½ inch of the top and bottom ends. Wrap in plastic and chill for at least 2 hours and up to 3 days. (For longer storage, it should go in the freezer.)

7. When ready to use, unwrap the dough, complete two last turns, and follow the directions in the main recipe for using the puff pastry.

Desserts

L'ÉBAUCHOIR

43-45, RUE DE CÎTEAUX
TEL: 01 43 42 49 31
MÉTRO: FAIDHERBE-CHALIGNY

Alarming rumors suggesting that L'Ébauchoir *gâteau de riz "grand-mère,"* a terrine of vanilla-scented rice pudding on a caramel bedding, is not like it used to be are, I'm happy to report, entirely unfounded. Nevertheless, the mere suggestion prompted me to seek out the recipe as insurance against such a catastrophe.

Finding itself on the short end of the secondhand *bavardage* (talk) that greatly influences Paris opinion is a new experience for this excellent bistro and its diligent chef, Thomas Dufour. Taking its name from a carpenter's tool, "The Chisel" was opened in 1991 as an economical lunch spot for the craftsmen employed in the many workshops near the Faubourg St-Antoine. As young artists and professionals began converting those workshops into lofts, L'Ébauchoir too gentrified itself— but not its decor, prices, or straightforward approach—by opening for dinner. When, three years later, a local critic named it the best bistro in Paris, the ensuing *bavardage* transformed a local haunt into a destination restaurant that could have easily been renamed after the favorite tool of the newcomers, *"Le Portable"*—the cellular phone.

The four-table terrace and pillared interior have the unfinished look of a sleepy Mediterranean café: green-gray plastered wainscoting, yellowish walls, old mirrors, Moorish tiles, woodcarvings and bric-a-brac, a few bookshelves. Cone-shaped lamps hang over the bar where fortyish intellectuals invariably wait for a table.

Though he cooked at the Michelin-three-starred Arpège, Dufour came to L'Ébauchoir in 1995 with no high-minded ideas about serving *gastro* cuisine. His focus has stayed fixed on doing the basics creatively with fresh herbs and vegetables purchased at the nearby place d'Aligre market. His cuisine possesses the flavor-focused simplicity and modest sophistication to which hundreds of phony contemporary bistros aspire. Wonderful Provençal seafood specials do not diminish the imperative of salmon *unilatéral*, a fixture on the blackboard menu matched in popularity only by the *gâteau de riz* and the creamy, dreamy *pot-de-crème vanille* (vanilla custard).

"If we take them off the menu, we're dead," says Dufour with weary resignation. "The *bavardage* would kill us."

L'ÉBAUCHOIR: Crisp Zucchini Sticks with Fennel (*page 54*), Sautéed Tuna Steak with Orange and Star Anise Butter Sauce (*page 66*), Rice Pudding "Grand-Mère" (*page 143*), Vanilla Custard (*page 150*)

RICE PUDDING "GRAND·MÈRE"

GÂTEAU DE RIZ GRAND·MÈRE

Publication of this rice pudding terrine reduces by one the number of essential reasons to visit Paris. Bring the terrine to the table, as they do at L'Ébauchoir, and let your guests help themselves to their preferred ratio of rice pudding top and caramel bottom.

1. Preheat oven to 450°F.

2. Heat the milk in a saucepan over medium-high heat and bring to a boil.

3. Clip off the ends of the vanilla beans, split open lengthwise, and scrape the grains. Add the vanilla beans and grains to the boiling milk, pour in the rice, lower the heat, and cook, stirring occasionally, for 40 minutes.

4. Meanwhile, combine ½ the sugar with the water in a heavy skillet and cook the mixture over high heat, stirring all the time with a wooden spoon and scraping down any sugar crystals clinging to the side of the pan. When the syrup is deep caramel in color, remove from the heat and pour in the bottom of a 1½-quart terrine, casserole, or loaf pan.

5. When the rice is nearly done, remove the vanilla beans. Combine the remaining ½ cup sugar and the eggs and beat with a whisk. Pour this mixture into the rice and mix well.

6. Pour the rice pudding into the terrine, place it directly on the bottom of the oven, and bake until the caramel begins to bubble up on the sides, about 10 minutes. Remove from the oven and let cool.

MAKES 6 SERVINGS

PREPARATION TIME:
5 MINUTES

COOKING TIME: 1 HOUR

5 cups milk

2 vanilla beans (or substitute 1 to 2 teaspoons vanilla extract)

½ cup long-grain rice

1 cup sugar

3 tablespoons water

2 large eggs, beaten

L'Été en Pente Douce

23, rue Muller
Tel: 01 42 64 02 67
Métro: Château-Rouge

It's not hard to imagine this picturesque café/*salon de thé,* with its shady cobblestone terrace, marble fireplace, Oriental rugs, and 1908 ceramic ornamentation, as a favored haunt of Picasso, Braque, and van Dongen at the storied time when modern art was in its infancy and Montmartre in its bohemian heyday. But L'Été en Pente Douce ("summer in gentle slope"), perched to the right and down seven flights of stairs from the Basilique du Sacré-Coeur, was named after a Gérard Krawczyk 1987 film and not opened until 1990. The space may have been a meeting point for Montmartre merchants and residents, as well as the rues Muller, Feurtrier, Utrillo, and Paul-

Albert, in its former life as a bakery. But now it is best characterized as the secluded, not excessively touristy place knowing Parisians go when entertaining guests from out of town.

Many of the locals who do use the café for daily routines, rendezvous, and situational interludes disappear as soon as they hear the springtime chirping of birds—and strangers. From winter to summer, the number of habitués in the café plummets as its volume jumps from 150 to 300 *couverts* (table settings). Yet anyone with free time during weekday mornings and afternoons in any season will encounter here one of the most quietly enchanting public hideaways in Paris.

Dinner, however, is another thing. To keep the wait for a table down to twenty minutes, Jean-Louis Spapperi, the enterprising proprietor, serves whole meals on a single plate. There are no appetizers listed atop his slate menu of thirteen main courses priced from 48 to 95 francs (about $8 to $16). Huge mixed salads and hearty dishes like stuffed duck *en croûte de sel* (cooked in a salted pastry), beef *tourte,* and Norwegian salmon in puff pastry encourage diners to eat the way the French think Americans do: double the food in half the time. So rushed a meal is contrary to the pleasures of even the most informal French dining.

Consequently, regulars ignore its chow off the chalkboard, as does chef Jean-Luc Brillet, who regards it as an advertisement to bring people in and is thus beneath him. Since his passion is wild mushrooms (ask him about *pleurotes* or *morilles* and he might answer you in under two hours), the trick is to order any *plat du jour* made with them. Otherwise, the breathtaking L'Été en Pente Douce can be a slippery slope.

LEMON TART WITH PRUNE PRESERVE

TARTE AU CITRON ET PRUNEAUX

A most agreeable departure from the classic lemon tart, with its thick layer of tangy lemon custard and thin layer of prune preserve not interacting until the critical moment when they leave your fork.

1. Preheat the oven to 400°F.

2. Butter a 9-inch tart tin. Roll out the pastry dough into a ⅛-inch-thick circle and line the tart tin with the dough. Poke the pastry dough with a fork in several spots. Refrigerate for 30 minutes.

3. Meanwhile, combine the prunes, water, and ¼ cup sugar in a saucepan over medium-low heat and cook until all the liquid is absorbed, about 30 minutes.

4. Line the chilled pastry shell with waxed paper and fill it with raw rice or dried beans to weigh it down. Bake for 10 minutes. Carefully remove the rice or beans and the waxed paper and continue to bake the piecrust for another 10 minutes. Remove from the oven and let cool.

5. Mash the prunes with a fork and spread evenly over the bottom of the shell.

6. Combine the eggs and remaining sugar and beat well with a whisk.

7. Melt the butter and combine it with the lemon zest and lemon juice. Add this to the egg mixture. Mix well and pour over the prunes in the tart shell.

8. Place the tart on the bottom shelf of the oven, lower the heat to 375°F, and bake until the top and edges are golden brown, 25 to 30 minutes. If the top browns too quickly, cover with aluminum foil.

MAKES 6 SERVINGS

PREPARATION TIME:
10 MINUTES (PLUS 1 HOUR
10 MINUTES FOR MAKING
THE DOUGH)

COOKING TIME: 1 HOUR
20 MINUTES

Unsalted butter for greasing the tart tin

1 recipe Pie Pastry (recipe follows)

1 cup pitted prunes, measured, then cut in half

½ cup water

1¼ cups sugar

2 large eggs

½ cup (1 stick) unsalted butter

Zest and juice of 2 lemons

PIE PASTRY

PÂTE BRISÉE

French for "short pastry" or "short paste," *pâte brisée* is the flaky pie dough most commonly used for tarts. Directions are given for making it both by hand and in a food processor.

BY HAND

1. Mix the flour and salt together in a large bowl.

2. Using a pastry blender, two knives, or your fingers, cut the butter into the flour until the mixture resembles a coarse meal.

3. Break up the vegetable shortening and add it in bits to the bowl. Continuing to use a pastry blender, two knives, or your fingers, cut in the shortening until the mixture becomes small clumps and curds.

4. Add the ice water and toss the mixture with a spatula until the water is incorporated.

5. Form the dough into a ball, roll it in flour, wrap it in waxed paper or plastic wrap, and chill it for at least 1 hour, or for up to several days, before using.

IN A FOOD PROCESSOR

1. Fit the food processor with the steel blade. Combine the flour, salt, butter, and vegetable shortening and process until the mixture resembles a coarse meal.

2. Sprinkle a little ice water into the mixture, pulse a few times, add more water, and pulse again until the mixture comes together in large pieces the size of pebbles.

3. Transfer the dough to a flat, lightly floured work surface and if the dough is dry, sprinkle it with another tablespoon of ice water. Form the dough into a ball, roll it in flour, wrap it in waxed paper or plastic wrap, and chill for at least 1 hour, or up to several days, before using.

MAKES ONE 9- TO 10-INCH TART SHELL

PREPARATION TIME: 10 MINUTES (PLUS AT LEAST 1 HOUR FOR REFRIGERATION)

1¼ cups flour, plus more for rolling the dough

¼ teaspoon salt

6 tablespoons (¾ stick) cold unsalted butter

2 tablespoons cold vegetable shortening

3 tablespoons ice water

DAME TARTINE

2, RUE BRISEMICHE
TEL: 01 42 77 32 22
MÉTRO: HÔTEL-DE-VILLE
59, RUE DE LYON
TEL: 01 44 68 96 95
MÉTRO: BASTILLE

A number of Parisians suffer from directional dyslexia. They are liable, for example, to pinpoint Dame Tartine as the café to the right of the Pompidou Center and directly opposite the Stravinsky Fountain instead of describing the Pompidou Center as the modern art museum to the left of Dame Tartine and the Stravinsky Fountain as the pool of colorfully sculptured creatures merrily spritzing its terrace.

Among her many virtues, Dame Tartine must yield credit to her neighbors in the Beaubourg quarter for providing the fountain-front vista and the rhythmic streams of people traffic. But its youthful sophistication, relaxed ambience, quick service, adorably plated meals, low prices, and innovative menu were inspired by Robert Petit and his vision of French fast food. Dame Tartine, as it turns out, is a not a lady at all.

Petit cooked for the gastronomical elite—Taillevent, Le Nôtre, Le Petit Colombier, Jacques Maximin—before storing away enough ideas and money, at the age of twenty-one, for a place of his own. His idea back in 1981 was to propose something that might slow the incursion of McDonald's into Paris. He devised a post-modern cuisine that could be served quickly, attractively, and cheaply and which, though grounded in tradition, would be easily accessible to a young clientele with little or no exposure to classic French cooking. Dishes with starter sets of contrasting flavors, colors, textures, and temperatures would be garnished with toast. (A *tartine* is a slice of bread or toast, with or without toppings.)

"I like contrast," explains Petit. "Hot–cold. Soft–hard. Bitter–sweet. I hate it when I put something in my mouth and nothing happens."

His plate of smoked salmon with chopped endive and ginger cream sauce provides lots of mouth action. The endive's bitter flavor is countered by the pungent aroma of the ginger, the smokiness of the salmon, and the sweetness of the cream. The crack of the chopped endive plays off the soft (but very different) textures of the smoked salmon and the cream. In another best-selling main course, a salmon trout fillet (pink) is garnished with lemon (yellow) and tomato (red) and served over saffron mashed potatoes (golden).

Petit does similarly cute, if rarely robust, adaptations with chicken, duck breast, and lamb. No main course is priced over 45 francs (about $7.50)! Yet his greatest passion is dessert. Observing that (a) most people dislike the flavor of chestnuts but that (b) the minority who like chestnuts love chestnuts, he (c) created *"marronnettes,"* a Bavarian pastry with chestnut overkill. Chestnut cake. Chestnut mousse. Chestnut cream. As a substitution for the ubiquitous (even in France) tiramisù, he designed an *"entremet de chocolat blanc,"* with layers of white chocolate mousse, espresso-soaked cake, and whipped cream drizzled with rum-flavored caramel. Wow! Either selection can keep fellow diners occupied while you monopolize Petit's sensational warm peach cake bottomed with strawberry sauce and topped with peach coulis. If these desserts were served with cloth napkins and silverware, presented on larger, more elegant plates, and garnished with ornate *cornets* (cream horns) and *florettes* and such-other-*ettes*, they would easily qualify as fine patisserie. Happily, they are presented rather modestly on small plates over paper placemats with 20-franc (about $3.30) price tags at one of the most glorious urban café terraces in Europe.

The rows of tables, chairs, and parasols along the wondrous Stravinsky Fountain invite, like Petit's dishes, lots of communication between different flavors, colors, and temperaments; 350,000 people rendezvous at Dame Tar-tine each year. Although a clientele so vast is difficult to characterize, it's apparent the café possesses a special allure for young women. Petit estimates that nearly 70 percent of his customers are women between the ages of fifteen and forty. French movie actresses Isabele Adjani and Juliette Binoche were regulars before they—and the café—got too popular. Director Eric Rohmer filmed a scene from *Les Rendez-vous de Paris* on the terrace and visits often, perhaps to lift some of the café dialogue so pervasive in his screenplays.

Some conversationalists prefer to sit indoors where there are fewer distractions in the lofty room save for the rotating art exhibitions and the view outside the casement windows. Still, it's not nearly as discreet as the thirty-seat Dame Tartine outpost which is not, as certain guides will tell you, near the Bastille. It is the Bastille that is near Dame Tartine.

DAME TARTINE: Fillet of Trout with Olive Oil-Creamed Potatoes (*page 99*), Warm Peach Cake with Two Sauces (*page 149*)

WARM PEACH CAKE WITH TWO SAUCES

Gâteau Chaud aux Pêches et des Deux Coulis

It's a cinch to prepare this superbly moist and buttery peach cake with the idea of eating one portion yourself and saving the rest for later. A successful *fin du coup* (follow-through) on that intention may, however, take years to master.

1. Preheat the oven to 375°F.

2. To prepare the cake batter and peach sauce, drain the syrup from the peaches and set aside for the peach sauce. Process the peaches in a food processor until smooth. Reserve ¾ of the pureed peaches (about 1½ cups) for the peach sauce. Pour the rest (about ⅜ cup) into a saucepan.

3. Add the butter to the saucepan and stir over medium heat until smooth.

4. Mix in the sugar and then, in order, the yeast, flour, beaten egg, and salt.

5. Butter a 6-inch-square cake pan and fill evenly with the cake batter. Bake for 20 minutes.

6. Meanwhile, in a small saucepan, combine the reserved syrup and peach puree to make the peach sauce. Set aside.

7. To prepare the strawberry sauce, combine the strawberries, confectioners' sugar, and water in a food processor and puree until smooth. Transfer to a saucepan.

8. Warm the two sauces separately.

9. To serve, cut the warm cake diagonally into 4 triangles. Spoon some warm peach sauce onto 4 dessert plates, place a triangle of cake on top of each, and then drape the warm strawberry sauce over the cake.

MAKES 4 SERVINGS

PREPARATION TIME:
15 MINUTES

COOKING TIME: 30 MINUTES

FOR CAKE BATTER AND
PEACH SAUCE

1 pound canned peaches in syrup

6 tablespoons (¾ stick) unsalted butter

3 tablespoons sugar

½ packet yeast, dissolved in warm water

⅓ cup flour

1 egg, beaten

A dash of salt

Unsalted butter for greasing cake pan

FOR STRAWBERRY SAUCE

10 ounces strawberries

⅓ cup confectioners' sugar

½ cup (scant) water

149

VANILLA CUSTARD

POT-DE-CRÈME VANILLE

Before all the crème brûlée brouhaha, there was the pristine, plain-as-vanilla pleasure of *pot-de-crème*.

1. Preheat the oven to 350°F.

2. In a saucepan, combine the milk and cream.

3. Clip off the ends of the vanilla beans, split them open lengthwise, and scrape out the grains. Add the beans and grains to the milk-cream mixture and heat to a boil.

4. Meanwhile, in a large bowl, combine the egg yolks and sugar and beat with a whisk.

5. Remove the vanilla beans from the boiling mixture, pour the liquid over the eggs, and beat with a whisk.

6. Pour this mixture into 6 ramekins and place them in a baking pan half filled with hot water.

7. Bake for 1 hour, remove from the baking pan, then let cool.

MAKES 6 SERVINGS

PREPARATION TIME:
5 MINUTES

COOKING TIME:
1 HOUR 10 MINUTES

2 cups milk

2 cups heavy cream

*2 or 3 vanilla beans
(or substitute 1 or 2
teaspoons vanilla extract)*

10 egg yolks

¾ cup sugar

LE VAUDEVILLE

29, RUE VIVIENNE
TEL: 01 40 20 04 62
MÉTRO: BOURSE

When Jean-Jacques Giraud, the decorous manager of Le Vaudeville, says there is just too much *"promiscuité"* in that high-styled Art Deco brasserie opposite the Bourse (the Paris Stock Exchange) for discreet deal making, he is not indicating, as English-speaking swingers are wont to misinterpret, an excessive amount of sexual activity in the routinely packed dining room. He means only that there are too many diverse interests and backgrounds sitting in close proximity for confidential conversation. Worse still, with journalists from the nearby headquarters of Agence France-Presse among the habitués, tonight's overheard whisper can turn quickly into the morning's front-page news.

The French meaning of *promiscuité* is, like the grand Parisian brasserie itself, the antithesis of privacy, calm, and exclusivity. It's what brings some morning cabbies and bankers, lunchtime stockbrokers, late-evening theater people, and anytime tourists to Le Vaudeville and no doubt keeps their more insular counterparts away. This is true even in the bar area that functions as a small canteen within the brasserie. The individuals who go to Café Beaubourg or Café de Flore for *petit déjeuner* instinctively spread themselves out as they would in a library reading room. A maître d' with a degree in landscaping could not do a better job of spacing the floor. At Le Vaudeville, the early risers congregate near one another. As early as 6 A.M., they want *promiscuité*. At lunch, up to twenty-five will elect to eat their daily chops, oysters, tartares, grilled fish, or lamb while standing at the bar.

Named for its long-ago demolished neighbor, the Théâtre le Vaudeville, the café-restaurant was renovated during the 1920s by A. L. and Paul Solvet, the interior designers of Montparnasse's La Coupole and Closerie de Lilas. By exalting these gathering places with the most sumptuous decoration of the Jazz Age, the Solvet brothers evidently understood then what I came to discover only after living in Paris for an extended period of time. Nothing in the city is so deserving of celebration as its routine pleasures. Le Vaudeville bestows everyday encounters with a backdrop of grand mirrors, marble walls, tubular bracket lamps, and bronze figures and bas-relief aligned in the geometric exuberance of Art Deco.

The menu at Le Vaudeville, now part of the Flo restaurant group, is rightly criticized as being too formulaic and sometimes indistinguishable from those of the other Flo brasseries. Still, I would go back anytime for the 169-franc (about $28) prix-fixe dinner menu that includes chef Jean-François Thorel's best appetizer, duck foie gras in Riesling-wine aspic; one of his finest main courses, grilled cod with truffle mashed potatoes; dessert; and a half bottle of wine. The Vaudeville supper menu, an after-theater special available from 10 P.M. until 2 A.M., offers the same minus the appetizer or dessert for 128 francs (about $21). The no-dessert option is not viable on summer nights, since there is no skipping the seasonal gratin of poached fresh figs draped in sabayon.

GRATIN OF FRESH FIGS
WITH A RED WINE SABAYON

GRATIN DE FIGUES FRAÎCHES, SABAYON AU VIN ROUGE

A midsummer night's dream: ripe figs poached in red wine and draped in a sensuous red-wine sabayon.

1. *The day before,* combine the wine, 1 cup of the sugar, and the cinnamon sticks in a saucepan and bring to a boil. Remove from the heat and set aside for 15 minutes.

2. Put the figs in a bowl, pour the wine over them, and cover. Refrigerate for 24 hours.

3. *The following day,* preheat the broiler.

4. Strain the wine from the figs into a saucepan. Set the figs aside.

5. Heat the wine over high heat until it is reduced to the consistency of a syrupy jelly, about 20 minutes.

6. Meanwhile, put the egg yolks and remaining sugar in the top of a double boiler over medium-high heat and beat with a whisk until smooth and creamy. Remove the pan from the heat and beat the sabayon for another 5 minutes.

7. Combine the heavy cream, confectioners' sugar, and vanilla extract in a mixing bowl and beat with a mixer or whisk into a whipped cream.

8. Immediately before serving, put the figs in a baking dish. Fold the whipped cream and reduced wine into the sabayon and pour over the figs. Put under the broiler until the sabayon is lightly browned, 2 to 4 minutes, and serve immediately in individual dishes.

MAKES 6 SERVINGS

PREPARATION TIME
(AFTER 24 HOURS POACHING):
10 MINUTES

COOKING TIME: 40 MINUTES

*1 liter full-bodied red wine
(such as Côté du Rhône)*

*1¼ cups plus 1 tablespoon
sugar*

3 sticks cinnamon

*18 fresh ripe figs, stemmed
and cut in half lengthwise*

5 large egg yolks

1 cup heavy cream

*2 tablespoons confectioners'
sugar*

1 teaspoon vanilla extract

COFFEE TART

TARTE AU CAFÉ

What better dessert for *The Paris Café Cookbook* than a coffee tart, especially one as terrific as this. Note that the tart must be chilled 12 hours before serving.

1. Grease a 9-inch round cake pan with the butter. Roll out the pastry dough. Line the pan with the dough and refrigerate for 30 minutes.

2. Preheat the oven to 320°F.

3. Line the chilled pastry with waxed paper and fill with raw rice, dry beans, or pie weights. Bake for 10 minutes. Carefully remove the rice, beans, or weights and the waxed paper and continue to bake the piecrust for 15 to 20 minutes, until golden brown. Cool.

4. Meanwhile, in a saucepan, combine the cream with the ground coffee and bring to a boil over medium-high heat. Immediately remove from the heat and steep for 5 minutes.

5. Melt the white chocolate in a double boiler and transfer to a large bowl.

6. In a large bowl, beat the egg yolk with the sugar until it is lemon-colored. Whisk in the cream-coffee mixture little by little and beat with a whisk until cool, about 5 minutes.

7. Pour the cream and egg yolk mixture into the melted chocolate, mixing well. Fold in the whipped cream.

8. Pour the mixture into the piecrust, cover, and refrigerate for 12 hours.

Note: Especially if it's warm in your kitchen, it helps to chill the bowl and beaters before you begin whipping the cream. You may also place the bowl of cream over a larger bowl filled with ice.

MAKES 6 SERVINGS

PREPARATION TIME:
25 MINUTES
(PLUS 1 HOUR 10 MINUTES
FOR MAKING THE DOUGH
AND 12 HOURS FOR
CHILLING THE BAKED TART)

COOKING TIME: 30 MINUTES

1 tablespoon unsalted butter

*1 recipe Pie Pastry
(page 146)*

½ cup heavy cream

*3 tablespoons freshly and
finely ground coffee*

6 ounces white chocolate

1 egg yolk

¼ cup sugar

*1 cup minus 2 tablespoons
heavy cream, whipped to
soft peaks (see Note)*

LE PETIT CHÂTEAU D'EAU

34, RUE CHÂTEAU-D'EAU
TEL: 01 47 70 11 00
MÉTRO: RÉPUBLIQUE

Being introduced to this or any obscure gem of a café is far more significant than the mode—newspaper blurb, personal recommendation—through which you learn of its existence. Still, I can't help feeling envious of the journalists at the daily *Libération* who in 1979 tripped upon Le Petit Château d'Eau while ambling past the wholesale clothing showrooms clustered on the side streets west of place de la République. The opening scenes of long-term relationships hold special meaning to café romantics. Their finding the café of their dreams by chance instead of by referral may be compared to spotting the love of one's life in that very café and not through a setup from a friend-of-a-friend-of-a-friend.

Though the zinc bar of this 1903 café was stripped off by German occupiers during World War II, as were bistro countertops throughout Paris, its beautiful beveled windows, floor mosaic, and Art Nouveau ceramics were left intact. Small groups of men invariably congregate at the far end of the semicircular mahogany bar. Solos and duos of either sex sit or stand nearer the window. Only owner Anne-Marie Monin, her son Nicolas, and waitresses Sylvie and Janine cross the invisible line between.

Since the folksy café closes immediately before dinner (8 or 9 P.M.), Nicolas calls it an "*apéro*"—short for *apéritif*—bar. Friends meet for drinks before going elsewhere to dine. At lunch, Le Petit Château d'Eau might instead be referred to as a *faux-filet* café. Local merchants, craftsmen, and journalists pack the cube-shaped café, tiny rear dining room, and sidewalk tables for the short selection of omelets, salad platters, a single plat du jour, a dependable fruit *clafoutis* (batter cake) du jour, and dependable *faux-filet*—the prized French counterpart to New York strip steak that is merely seasoned with salt and pepper and pan-fried in butter. Contrary to romanticized imagery, a good steak, as much as croissants and café au lait, can make a café.

PEAR CLAFOUTI

Clafoutis aux Poires

Few baked desserts are simpler or more foolproof than a clafouti, a soft batter cake traditionally filled with black cherries. But you may instead use prunes, plums, berries, apples, or, following this recipe, pears.

1. Preheat the oven to 375°F.

2. Put all of the ingredients except the pears and butter in a large bowl and beat well with a whisk.

3. Add the pears and mix well with a spoon.

4. Butter a baking dish about 9 inches round and at least 2 inches high and pour in the batter, being sure that the pears are flattened down and well distributed.

5. Bake for 40 minutes, or until puffed and golden brown. Cut like a tart into triangular slices, and serve warm on individual plates.

MAKES 6 SERVINGS

PREPARATION TIME:
10 MINUTES

COOKING TIME: 40 MINUTES

1 cup flour

1 tablespoon vanilla extract

1/3 cup sugar

3 large eggs

1 cup milk

1/2 cup heavy cream

A pinch of salt

5 pears, peeled and cut into 1/4-inch slices

Unsalted butter for greasing baking dish

CHOCOLATE PROFITEROLES

PROFITEROLES AU CHOCOLAT

If the chocolate sauce is served tepid, these classic ice cream–filled puffs can rank with the fallen soufflé among the great tragedies in the French dessert experience. At brasseries and bistros, the hot sauce is traditionally brought to the table in a silver pitcher and poured directly over the *choux* puffs by the garçon. At home, the time from when the sauce leaves the double boiler to when it reaches its final destination should be kept under a half minute. As a substitute for the melted chocolate topping below, Café de Flore's thick hot chocolate (halve the recipe on page 163) will produce gorgeous results if served in 29 seconds or less. Anything longer, *c'est une catastrophe*.

MAKES 6 SERVINGS (3 CHOUX PER PLATE)

PREPARATION TIME: 20 MINUTES (PLUS 15 MINUTES FOR MAKING THE PASTRY)

COOKING TIME: 30 MINUTES

Unsalted butter for greasing the baking sheet

2 1/2 cups Choux Paste (page 45)

8 ounces semisweet or bittersweet chocolate, broken into pieces

1/4 cup whole milk

1 pint vanilla ice cream

1. Preheat the oven to 425°F.

2. Butter a baking sheet. Make 1 1/2-inch balls of pastry dough and lay them out on the baking sheet in one of two ways: either fill a pastry bag and pipe out the puffs or simply use one teaspoon to gather the pastry and another to push it onto the baking sheet.

3. Brush the tops carefully with beaten egg (remaining from preparing the *choux* paste). Bake in the oven until golden and puffed to about double their original size, about 20 minutes. Turn off the oven and leave the pastries in for another 10 minutes with the door ajar. Remove from the oven and let cool.

4. Before serving, put the chocolate and the milk in a double boiler over medium-high heat, and cook until the chocolate is melted, stirring with a wooden spoon. Keep warm.

5. Carefully halve the puffs, fill the bottoms with a small scoop of vanilla ice cream and replace the tops. Place 3 on each plate and douse with melted chocolate. Serve within 29 seconds.

TARTE TATIN

MAKES 6 SERVINGS

PREPARATION TIME:
15 MINUTES (PLUS 4 HOURS
FOR MAKING THE DOUGH)

COOKING TIME:
1 HOUR 15 MINUTES

Pale, undercaramelized tarte Tatins (upside-down apple tarts) are the scourge of Paris. There is hope for future generations in this basic rendition.

1. Preheat the oven to 400°F.

2. Melt ½ the butter (¼ cup) in a 9-inch oven-proof frying pan over high heat. Add the sugar and stir with a wooden spoon until the mixture becomes syrupy and reaches a light caramel color. Remove from the heat.

3. Arrange the apple slices atop the caramel in a tight spiral (or concentric circles) to cover the bottom of the pan. Scatter any remaining apple slices to form a second layer on top.

4. Cut the remaining butter into small cubes, dot the apples, and bake for 35 minutes. Remove from the oven and let cool.

5. Roll out the pastry to a round sheet about a little more than ⅛ inch in thickness and an inch wider than the top of the pan. Place the pastry sheet over the apples and press the edges down around the inside rim of the pan.

6. Bake the tart for an additional 35 minutes.

7. Turn a serving dish over the tart and flip them both over to unmold the tart. In the likely event that some apple slices are left behind in the pan, rearrange them atop the tart.

8. Serve warm with crème fraîche, whipped cream, or vanilla ice cream.

½ cup (1 stick) unsalted butter

1 cup sugar

6 apples (preferably Golden Delicious), peeled, cored, and quartered

1 pound puff pastry (page 138)

Crème fraîche (page 17), whipped cream, or vanilla ice cream

Tarte Tatin

157

PEACH AND NECTARINE SOUP WITH A SAUCE OF RED BERRIES AND FRESH MINT

Soupe de Pêches et Nectarines,

Coulis de Fruits Rouges et Menthe Fraîche

This dessert soup may be served warm or chilled. A scoop or two of fruit sorbet would do no harm.

1. Puree the berries, confectioners' sugar, and lemon juice together in a food processor until smooth, about 2 minutes. Pass through a strainer to remove the seeds. Set aside.

2. Put the water, sugar, and ½ the mint leaves in a large saucepan and bring to a boil.

3. Add the peaches and nectarines to the water-and-sugar mixture and poach for 3 minutes.

4. Remove the peaches and nectarines from the liquid and peel them. Remove the pits and cut the fruit into quarters.

5. Add the berry syrup to the simple syrup (sugar and water) and heat until reduced by half. Pour through a strainer to remove the mint leaves.

6. Divide the peaches and nectarines among 4 soup dishes and ladle the fruit soup on top. Cut the remaining fresh mint leaves into thin strips and scatter over the soup.

MAKES 4 SERVINGS

PREPARATION TIME:
20 MINUTES

COOKING TIME: 35 MINUTES

1½ pounds raspberries, blackberries, and/or strawberries

1 cup confectioners' sugar

1 teaspoon fresh lemon juice

1 quart water

1 cup sugar

1 bunch fresh mint

3 peaches, unpeeled

3 nectarines, unpeeled

BOUILLON RACINE

3, RUE RACINE

TEL: 01 46 34 55 22

MÉTRO: CLUNY-SORBONNE, SAINT-MICHEL

The December 1996 opening of Bouillon Racine, a Belgian café that restored a Latin Quarter landmark to its fin-de-siècle splendor, could easily have been received as a generous Christmas gift by Left Bank traditionalists. But so far, chef/proprietor Olivier Simon has received few *remerciements,* to be narrowly interpreted as "thank-yous" of French, as opposed to Belgian or Anglo, origin.

The term *bouillon* here refers to the soup counters first opened at the doors of nineteenth-century butchers. By 1880, there were 150 *bouillons* serving Parisian workers. Soon a new wave of more elaborate, café-styled *bouillons* began serving a bourgeois clientele. Among them was the Grand Bouillon Camille Chartier, whose beauty, owing to Simon, may now be seen in person and not just in photos. Ornate Art Nouveau woodwork with exquisitely painted floral inlays was stripped down to its original—and astonishing—circa 1906 celery-green color. The remaining patch of a mosaic floor composed of the finest marbles was faithfully reproduced throughout the café.

So as not to be viewed as a museum by the locals it wishes to lure back to this address, namely, students and faculty from the Sorbonne and editors from nearby publishing houses, the ground floor was decorated with contemporary iron tables, chairs, and lighting fixtures alluding to the organic designs typical of Art Nouveau. The additions were seized by certain Parisians as another opportunity to disparage the Belgians. Even the most positive word of mouth regarding Bouillon Racine invariably includes disapproval of the new furniture.

There are few other decisions to criticize. The café carries Mariage Frère teas, Illy espresso, and Belgian beers that even the most chauvinistic Frenchmen will concede are far superior to theirs. Its calm afternoon service is configured as a *"salon de thé et bière."* The menu, printed on a monthly newsletter promoting Belgian cultural events, displays the richness of a cuisine that goes well beyond the traditional *moules-frites* (mussels and fries). The fine meat and fish dishes that Simon, an accomplished chef, cooks in beer reflect the sweet-and-sour character of much Belgian cuisine. A soup *bouillon* is an indispensable feature, as is the authentically creamy *café liégeois,* a treat Belgian in name if not origin of iced coffee, ice cream, and whipped cream that is a Paris café classic. For that alone some more Parisians should say, *"Merci, Monsieur Simon."*

CAFÉ LIÉGEOIS

The classic dessert beverage and old café standard consists of iced coffee combined with ice cream and whipped cream. While other cafés concoct frilly renditions that can resemble an ice cream parlor's coffee-float extravaganzas, Bouillon Racine serves a creamy, well-blended, no-nonsense *café liégeois*—just what you'd expect from the Paris café that seems to share with the drink a Belgian background. Its origin is actually Viennese.

1. Remove the ice cream from the freezer and let it soften a few minutes.

2. Meanwhile, using a whisk or electric beater, whip the heavy cream, slowly increasing the speed and adding the confectioners' sugar and vanilla extract, until soft peaks form.

3. Pour ½ cup of the iced coffee into each of 4 dessert glasses or coffee mugs. Add to each a scoop of ice cream and a dollop of whipped cream. Stir well and serve.

MAKES 4 SERVINGS

1 pint coffee ice cream

1 cup heavy cream

2 tablespoons confectioners' sugar

2 teaspoons vanilla extract

2 cups strong iced coffee

STRAWBERRY SOUP

NAGE DE FRAISES

In Bruno Neveu's enchanting strawberry "soup" (*nage* means "swimming"), the raspberries, blackberries, and red currants serve as decoration. You may therefore alter the quantities and proportions.

1. Combine the orange juice and anisette liqueur in a bowl, add the strawberries, and refrigerate for 1 hour.

2. Immediately before serving, divide the juice and strawberries among 4 small soup bowls, and decorate each bowl with a quarter of the raspberries, blackberries, and red currants, and a few mint leaves.

MAKES 4 SERVINGS

PREPARATION TIME
(AFTER CHILLING FOR
1 HOUR): 2 MINUTES

*2 cups freshly squeezed
    orange juice*

*¼ cup anisette liqueur
    (Marie Brizard,
    Sambuca)*

*1½ cups strawberries,
    measured, then halved*

¼ cup raspberries

¼ cup blackberries

¼ cup red currants

1 bunch fresh mint

CAFÉ DE FLORE

172, BOULEVARD ST-GERMAIN
TEL: 01 45 48 55 26
MÉTRO: ST-GERMAIN-DES-PRÉS

The literary Eden of the St-Germain-des-Prés district, Café de Flore ("Flora") has nurtured three great "isms" of the twentieth century: surrealism, existentialism, and tourism. During the years immediately before World War I, Guillaume Apollinaire, the poet and art critic said to have coined the term *surrealism,* held court with his cohorts at the window table tucked between the iron-framed glass vestibule and the winding stairway. In 1939, novelist and feminist Simone de Beauvoir introduced existentialist Jean-Paul Sartre to the Flore. The lifelong companions hibernated with their fellow "-ists" in the warmth of the café during the harsh winters of the World War II years. Sartre did some of his finest writing at the café's tables, too much of it if you asked proprietor Paul Boubal.

"Sartre became my worst client," Boubal complained. "He would stay for hours, scribbling on paper over a single drink that from morning to night was never refreshed."

Luminaries and lesser lights can still loiter all day long on a single coffee, only it will cost them 23 francs (about $3.75)—a hefty sum to dish out for a cup of java whose capacity to unclog writer's block has never been proven. What they're paying for is a seat in a mecca of people-watching and exhibitionism. The terrace rows of red-and-green caned chairs all face out as if the constricted view of traffic-congested St-Germain was that of moviedom converging on Cannes' boulevard de la Croisette. But total café glamour, whether at the Flore or on the French Riviera, is in being on the inside appearing to look out, but actually sneaking sideways glances from behind dark sunglasses. The outward vista is irrelevant.

So too seems the entire spectacle to the white-collar intellectuals who climb to the Flore's upper level. Their esteem for the dining room they employ as an office is the most deliciously contradictory conceit in the Paris café experience. They eschew the heady excitement of the bright, elegant, storied space below for the club-like seclusion upstairs which, despite its window flora, is stuffy and completely shut off from the action. Assuming one is a proponent of relativism, then finding privacy and calm in so public and touristy a place is apt to have a singular appeal. It may even justify splurging for ham and eggs, a decent club sandwich, or a world-class hot chocolate—all madly overpriced. At the beloved Flore, better than being on the outside looking in or on the inside looking out is to be above it all.

HOT CHOCOLATE

CHOCOLAT CHAUD

Peeking behind the cashier's booth into the Flore's narrow kitchen, you can see, to the immediate left, its most essential appliance: a tall double boiler with a built-in stirring mechanism that keeps the café's thicker-than-thick, richer-than-rich, darker-than-dark *chocolat* at the hot and ready. Poured by the garçon from a small silver pitcher into the Flore's elegant coffee cup, it is less a hot dessert beverage than a chocolate heat rub for the inner soul. *Impressionnant!*

MAKES 4 CUPS

COOKING TIME: 10 MINUTES

7 ounces bittersweet chocolate (hard), broken into small pieces

2 cups cold milk

⅔ cup heavy cream

1 teaspoon vanilla extract

DOUBLE BOILER DIRECTIONS

1. Put the chocolate and ¼ cup of the cold milk in a double boiler over medium-high heat and cook until the chocolate is melted, stirring with a wooden spoon.

2. Add the rest of the milk and the cream and vanilla extract and heat, stirring constantly, until hot and fully blended.

SAUCEPAN DIRECTIONS

1. Put the chocolate and ½ cup of the cold milk in a saucepan, cover, and cook over low heat until the chocolate has softened, about 3 minutes. The milk must never be allowed to boil. Remove from the heat and whip with a whisk until smooth.

2. Add the remaining milk and the cream and vanilla extract and cook over medium heat, stirring all the time with a wooden spoon, until hot and fully blended.

CREPES

This recipe is adapted from the formula given to me by Joseph Karad-eniz, who leased the crepe stand outside the café. You may prepare all the crepes in advance, stacking them flat in a covered dish, keeping them warm in a low oven, and not applying any toppings until you're ready to serve. My favorite filling is the sweet combination of half a banana thinly sliced and 2 tablespoons of Nutella hazelnut chocolate spread.

1. Put the flour in a large bowl and make a well in the center.

2. Break the eggs into the well in the flour. Add 1 cup of the milk to the eggs and stir in a circular motion with a wooden spatula, gradually widening the circle to incorporate a little flour at a time until all the flour is absorbed by the liquid.

3. Add the remaining ½ cup milk and the water, sugar, melted butter, and salt and beat with a whisk until all the lumps have disappeared. (If you can't eliminate them all, pour the batter through a strainer.) Let the batter stand 1 hour in the refrigerator.

4. Put the vegetable oil into a 9-inch crepe pan or skillet and heat over medium heat. Ladle ¼ cup of the batter into the pan, then quickly tilt the pan in all directions so the batter spreads into a thin layer covering the bottom of the pan. Cook the crepe until the bottom is lightly browned and the edges lift up easily from the pan, about 2 minutes.

5. Slide a spatula under the crepe and, grabbing the opposite side with your fingers, flip it over.

6. Spread the desired fillings over the center of the crepe and cook the underside until it becomes brown spotted, about 1 minute. To finish, fold it three times into a rounded triangle: First fold it in half over the fillings, then fold the resulting semicircle in thirds, making two creases with the side of the spatula to ease the folding.

MAKES ABOUT
16 CREPES

PREPARATION TIME:
10 MINUTES (PLUS 1 HOUR
TO CONDITION THE BATTER)

COOKING TIME: 25 MINUTES

2 cups flour

3 eggs

1½ cups milk

½ cup water

*2 tablespoons sugar
    (for dessert crepes only)*

*2 tablespoons unsalted
    butter, melted*

Pinch of salt

1 tablespoon vegetable oil

*Fillings (ham and cheese,
    jams, bananas, chestnut
    butter, Nutella)*

LE SANCERRE

35, RUE DES ABBESSES
TEL: 01 42 58 08 20
MÉTRO: ABBESSES

Once established as the Montmartre rendezvous of bikers and bankers, conformists and originals, performing artists and pickup artists, professional models and full-time poseurs, Le Sancerre could have dropped the idea of also attracting that fringe group of the Pigalle populace best identified as diners. Other raucous cafés aspiring to the same measure of coolness make not the slightest effort to serve decent grub.

That's a pity in a city where good food products can be more convenient than inferior ones. Evidence of that fact stares you right in the face when you're seated out on one of Le Sancerre's long, caned banquettes and see the cheese store, butcher, fruit stand, and delicatessen across the cobblestone street.

Owner Boris Ballay, who bought the café in 1990 and installed its stainless-steel bar, jazz photos, and toy alligator mascot, spares his clientele the agony of eating poorly in such appetizing surroundings. His paper place mat and blackboard menus list good *tartines*, substantial salads and cheese and charcuterie platters, above-average steaks, and a commendable apple crumble. At lunch, the café is less a bar than a reliable, inexpensive bistro that, in the heart of Montmartre, inserts the beat of the current *fin de siècle* into the heart of the prior one.

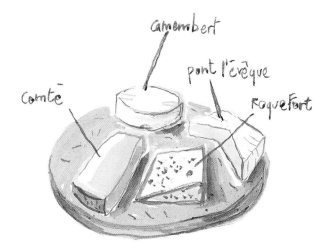

APPLE CRUMBLE

The greatest contribution to the Paris café menu from the British Isles since Welsh rarebit, fruit crumbles are all the rage in modest bistros, refined tea salons, and even deluxe, multistarred restaurants throughout the French capital as diners crave the reassuring comfort of desserts that look and taste homemade. Café and home cooks shouldn't mind satisfying these urges, since crumbles, English cousins to American cobblers and crisps, are much easier to prepare than traditional fruit tarts and pies. Without the bother of a short or puff pastry, the raw fruit filling requires only a crumb topping before being baked. On café menus like the one printed on Le Sancerre's paper place mat, "Apple Crumble" is rarely if ever translated into French.

1. Preheat the oven to 375°F.

2. Toss the apples with the white sugar, lemon juice, and cinnamon and put them into a buttered 1½-quart baking dish.

3. Sift the flour and light brown sugar together into a bowl, and cut in the butter, using a pastry blender, two knives, or your fingers, until it resembles coarse crumbs.

4. Toss with the nuts, spread evenly over the apples, and bake until the crust is browned, about 45 minutes.

5. Serve hot or let cool.

MAKES 4 TO 6 SERVINGS

PREPARATION TIME: 10 MINUTES

COOKING TIME: 45 MINUTES

6 tart apples (Granny Smith or Golden Delicious), peeled, cored, and sliced

½ cup white sugar

Juice of ½ lemon

1 teaspoon ground cinnamon

Unsalted butter for greasing the baking dish

1½ cups flour

½ cup light brown sugar

½ cup (1 stick) unsalted butter

½ cup chopped walnuts, almonds, or hazelnuts

ZÉPHYR

1, RUE DU JOURDAIN
TEL: 01 46 36 65 81
MÉTRO: JOURDAIN

"It's easy to choose a great wine," remarks Patricia Laloum, the co-owner of Zéphyr and co-producer of its eclectic wine list. "Choosing a small wine is not so simple."

The same rule applies to Parisian dining decisions. Settling upon a celebrated restaurant like Lucas-Carton or Taillevent takes lots of money but very little effort and know-how. Choosing a modest, out-of-the-way brasserie like Zéphyr depends on the reverse requirements. Those who fulfill them are rewarded in finding this Montparnasse-like Art Deco gem quietly tucked away in Haut-Belleville, a residential neighborhood in northwest Paris where young artists and creative professionals are taking refuge. The relaxed cadence and casual sophistication of Zéphyr's bar, dining room, and terrace epitomize their ideal of escaping the city without actually leaving it.

Ironically, Zéphyr was for over fifty years a stuck-up dining establishment that closed off its haute cuisine from Haut-Belleville with two sets of curtains and double-glazed windows. Laloum and her partner in business and life, Méziane Azaïche, were despised as renegades by the old habitués when they took down those curtains, relaxed the prices and dress code, and exposed the fluted woodwork, decorative-glass panels and sconces, and geometric broken-tile mosaics by the renowned Hazard to a wider audience. Today, the hard-working yet easygoing Azaïche, an Algerian immigrant who also revived the theater troupe Cabaret Sauvage, is adored as a community treasure.

The menu too is more democratic than before. Chef Stephane Baron is a devotee of *cuisine du marché* (market cuisine). His daily specials are inspired less by ego than by what catches his eye at the Rungis wholesale market. He groups together *nouvelle* inspirations like tabouleh salad with artichokes, grapefruit, and fresh mint; salmon carpaccio scented with vanilla; and a fricassee of young rabbit with sour cherries and ginger alongside classics such as *pot-au-feu, blanquette de veau,* and *confit de canard.*

Baron makes it easier for a diner to choose a great dessert than a small one. During summer, proof is in the white peach frozen parfait, the frozen nougat with mango coulis, and the crème brûlée perfumed on a whim with chocolate-mint, honey-lemon, rhubarb, or even classic vanilla.

ZÉPHYR: Vegetable Terrine with Vinaigrette (*page 29*), Crème Brûlée (*page 168*)

CRÈME BRÛLÉE

After a few weeks of such flavored crème brûlées as sweet-and-tart honey-lemon and dynamite-delicious chocolate-mint with melted chocolate on the bottom of the baking dish, I think you'll conclude that classic vanilla is still the best. Nevertheless, so that you can test this thesis as frequently and thoroughly as possible, I've included the honey-lemon and chocolate-mint versions as well.

1. Preheat the oven to 325°F.

2. Pour the heavy cream into a saucepan. Clip off the ends of the vanilla beans, split them open lengthwise, and scrape out the grains. Add the beans and grains to the cream and heat to a boil. Remove from the heat and let cool.

3. In a large bowl, beat the egg yolks and the sugar together with a whisk until whitened. Top with the cream and beat just to combine.

4. Strain the custard (removing the vanilla beans) into six 1-cup baking dishes, place in a baking pan filled with a ½ inch of hot water, and bake for 30 minutes.

5. Remove from the oven, let cool, and then refrigerate for at least 30 minutes.

6. Preheat the broiler.

7. First blot any liquid from the top of the custard, then sift the ½ cup sugar evenly over the custards to a thickness of about ¼ inch.

8. Place on the top shelf of the broiler and let the sugar caramelize until brown, 2 to 3 minutes, checking often so that the sugar does not burn. Remove and let chill for at least 5 minutes.

MAKES 6 SERVINGS

PREPARATION TIME:
10 MINUTES
(PLUS 30 MINUTES TO SET
CUSTARD AND TO CHILL
AFTER CARAMELIZING)

COOKING TIME: 40 MINUTES

1 quart heavy cream

2 vanilla beans

8 egg yolks

*5 tablespoons sugar, plus
½ cup for the caramel
topping*

Honey-Lemon Crème Brûlée: Prepare as on page 168, only use just 1 vanilla bean, and substitute 3 tablespoons strongly perfumed honey and the juice of 2 lemons for 3 tablespoons of the sugar.

Chocolate-Mint Crème Brûlée: Prepare as on page 168, with the following changes:

1. Heat the cream with only 1 vanilla bean, and after removing from the heat, add 3 sprigs of fresh mint to steep as the cream cools.

2. Add 2 teaspoons crème de menthe to the custard mixture.

3. Before pouring the mint-infused custard into the baking dishes, put a thin layer of shaved or grated dark chocolate (in total, about 3 ounces) on the bottom of each dish.

4. For the caramel topping, use light brown sugar.

CHOCOLATE MOUSSE

MOUSSE AU CHOCOLAT

A classic chocolate mousse richened with egg yolks and puffed with beaten egg whites.

1. In a saucepan, heat the chocolate and light cream over low heat, stirring occasionally with a wooden spoon, until the chocolate is fully melted. Remove from the heat and beat the egg yolks into the mixture, one at a time.

2. In a bowl, beat the egg whites with an electric mixer or whisk until stiff. Add the sugar slowly, beating as you go, and beat until the meringue holds stiff peaks.

3. Delicately stir the meringue mixture into the chocolate until fully incorporated.

4. Pour into 4 dessert bowls or glasses and refrigerate for at least 1 hour.

MAKES 4 SERVINGS

PREPARATION TIME:
15 MINUTES (PLUS
1 HOUR FOR CHILLING)

COOKING TIME: 3 MINUTES

7½ ounces dark chocolate, shaved or chopped

½ cup light cream

3 egg yolks

5 egg whites

3 tablespoons plus 1 teaspoon sugar

170

Chez Léon

5, RUE DE L'ISLY
TEL: 01 43 87 42 77
MÉTRO: SAINT-LAZARE

The tire-shaped, red-and-blue placard hanging on an obscure block near the Saint-Lazare train station is a familiar welcome sign on French provincial roads but unique to the streets of central Paris. Motorists recognize it as the emblem of Les Routiers, a national network of reliable roadside eateries first sanctioned to welcome truck drivers with good food at a good price. Chez Léon's conversion in 1950 from a typical bistro into Paris's sole *routier* was motivated by the traffic in and out of the nearby headquarters of the French truckers' union. Its raison d'être is now sustained by municipal workers, students, and travelers whose appetites are in solidarity with the truckers'.

In a frenzied district that recently has resembled one big construction site, Odette Grange, her son Christian, and her daughter Catherine run a warm refuge of reassuring continuity. To this family of Savoyarde origin (not every

bistro clan, it turns out, is from Auvergne) you must add waitresses Colette and Madeleine and barman René. Colette qualifies via marriage; dear Madeleine and affable René, through a combined fifty-four years of service. Regardless of what Christian accomplishes in the kitchen with such traditional plats du jour as *pot-au-feu*, *blanquette de veau* (veal stew), and *hachis parmentier* (shepherd's pie), this capable cook will always be admired by the habitués and newcomers sharing communal tables and conversations for his golden, hand-cut french fries and his Friday roast beef special. I admire too his fruit compotes, especially combos like apple-rhubarb and apple-quince.

The original bistro decor, said to have been quite attractive, was replaced by Formica counters and cabinetry in a hideous scheme of black and yellow. The 1950s design is now old enough to hold a retro, kitschy fascination. All that remains from before is the broken-tile mosaic floor and a wood cabinet with sixty-three numbered drawers in which regulars may store their personal cloth napkins. Sadly, this once-common custom endures in only a few choice bistros.

APPLE COMPOTE

COMPOTE DE POMMES

A compote is a comforting if unglamorous dessert of fresh or dried fruit stewed in sugar and water. Chez Léon's lunch menu features a compote *du jour*, usually consisting of apples either solo or in duet with rhubarb, quinces, or raisins.

Combine all the ingredients in a saucepan over high heat, stirring occasionally, until the compote has the consistency of thick applesauce, about 15 minutes. Serve hot or cold.

VARIATIONS

Apple-Rhubarb Compote: Substitute ⅔ pound rhubarb stalks (washed, trimmed, peeled, and cut into 1-inch pieces) for 3 of the apples and all of the water.

Apple-Quince Compote: Substitute 1 pound quinces (peeled, quartered, and cored) for 3 of the apples and increase the quantity of sugar by ¼ cup.

Apple-Raisin Compote: Add ½ cup raisins.

MAKES 4 SERVINGS

PREPARATION TIME: 5 MINUTES

COOKING TIME: 15 MINUTES

6 apples (preferably a tart variety such as Granny Smith), peeled, cored, and sliced

¾ cup sugar

1 cup cold water

Zest of 1 lemon

WEB BAR

32, RUE DE PICARDIE
TEL: 01 42 72 66 55
MÉTRO: RÉPUBLIQUE

The very concept of a cyber café, where strangers connect via modems and not eye contact, defies the cinematic quality of the Parisian café encounters affectionately portrayed in the films of Truffaut, Godard, Rohmer, and Sautet. Indeed, the scenario that has the seductively moody café hero passing up a seat opposite an unattended Juliette Binoche—or her look-alike—for one opposite an unattended IBM—or its clone—portends the death of the ever-looming café romance, if not French cinema itself.

Happily, the outcome of Web Bar, one of several cyber cafés in Paris, is not only ironic but very reassuring. With two modes of interaction competing for our attention, the chat groups on the "Web" have proven much less a draw than those at the "bar." A number of students, architects, journalists, and new-media artists do use the balconied computer stations that surround this skylit industrial loft, but many more prefer to congregate around the leather sofas, lounge chairs, and concrete blocks that furnish the airy café below.

The blueprint for a café interfacing art and technology was drawn up by Steve Gabison, an aeronautics engineer who helped design the autopilots for the wide-bodied Airbus 340. Befitting a background in commercial aviation, his designs placed as high a value on air space as cyber space while downplaying food.

Web Bar nevertheless has an appealing menu featuring homemade savory tarts, combination platters and salads, a selection of *bruschetta* assembled atop *pain Poilâne*, fruit crumbles, and a good chocolate cake. The daily lunch special offers a plat du jour and a choice of either an appetizer or a dessert. Most men, I'm told, take an appetizer; most women opt for dessert. The house Merlot is bottled with the private label of "Cuvée Web." The house cocktail, "Le Web," is mixed with one part Cointreau, two parts Campari, and two parts pink grapefruit juice.

As for the café-style cinema verité at the Web Bar, I'm glad to testify it's alive and well, if at times frustrating. During one lunch I exchanged looks and then some promising dialogue with Anne, an alluring journalist seated at the next table, only to let her slip away without getting her phone number or E-mail address. I've returned to that very table no more than fifteen times in the hopes of accidentally running into her, but so far, no Anne. You only find (or refind) the woman of your life, goes the café wisdom, when you stop looking.

CHOCOLATE CAKE

FONDANT AU CHOCOLAT

A *fondant au chocolat* is a cake that *fond*—"melts"—in the mouth. It is therefore no misdemeanor to slightly underbake it, resulting in a molten center of dark chocolate. Wedges of this intensely rich cake may be served alone, with a scoop of vanilla ice cream, or topped with hot chocolate sauce.

1. Preheat the oven to 325°F.

2. Butter and flour a 9-inch round cake pan. Line the bottom of the pan with buttered parchment paper or waxed paper.

3. Melt the chocolate in a double boiler, stir in the rum, and remove from the heat.

4. In a mixing bowl, with a whisk or an electric beater, cream the butter and sugar together until fluffy. Add the eggs and flour, 2 eggs and 1 heaping tablespoon flour at a time, beating well after each addition. Add the melted chocolate and mix well.

5. Pour the batter into the cake pan and place in a larger baking pan half filled with hot water.

6. Bake for 1 hour, testing to see if a toothpick comes out clean.

7. Serve hot or let cool in the pan for 5 minutes before turning out onto racks.

MAKES 8 SERVINGS

PREPARATION TIME:
10 MINUTES

COOKING TIME:
1 HOUR 10 MINUTES

Unsalted butter and flour for the cake pan

12 ounces semisweet chocolate, grated or broken into small pieces

1 teaspoon rum (optional)

1¼ cups (2½ sticks) unsalted butter

1 cup sugar

6 eggs

½ cup flour

INDEX

INDEX